jim croce

piano • vocal • guitar

the stories behind the songs

by Ingrid Croce

ISBN 978-1-4234-8302-1

7777 W. BLUEMOUND RD. P.O. BOX 13819 MILWAUKEE, WI 53213

For all works contained herein:
Unauthorized copying, arranging, adapting, recording, Internet posting, public performance,
or other distribution of the printed music in this publication is an infringement of copyright.
Infringers are liable under the law.

Visit Hal Leonard Online at
www.halleonard.com

Visit Jim Croce Official site at
www.jimcroce.com

the stories behind the songs

by Ingrid Croce

Table of Contents

4	**INTRODUCTION**
6	**THE STORIES BEHIND THE SONGS**
26	**JIM CROCE, "IN HIS OWN WORDS"**
28	Age
32	Alabama Rain
36	Bad, Bad Leroy Brown
40	Ballad of Gunga Din
48	Big Wheel
51	Box Number 10
56	Careful Man
59	Child of Midnight
64	Dreamin' Again
69	Five Short Minutes
74	Got No Business Singing the Blues
76	Hard Time Losin' Man
82	The Hard Way Every Time
79	Hey Tomorrow
86	I Am Who I Am
92	I Got a Name
89	I'll Have to Say I Love You in a Song
96	It Doesn't Have to Be That Way
100	Lover's Cross
110	Mary Ann
105	New York's Not My Home
114	(Next Time), This Time
117	One Less Set of Footsteps
122	Operator (That's Not the Way It Feels)
126	Pa
132	Photographs and Memories
134	Rapid Roy (The Stock Car Boy)
129	Recently
140	Roller Derby Queen
144	Speedball Tucker
147	These Dreams
150	Time in a Bottle
154	Tomorrow's Gonna Be a Brighter Day
164	Top Hat Bar and Grille
159	Vespers
168	Walkin' Back to Georgia
174	What Do People Do
171	Which Way Are You Goin'
178	Workin' at the Car Wash Blues
184	You Don't Mess Around with Jim

*Special thanks to Tania Garcia for additional editing
and to Ben Welch and Jeff Schroedl for all of their help and support.*

introduction
"the stories behind the songs"
by Ingrid Croce

When I'm asked, "Was there really a Bad, Bad Leroy Brown?" or "Do you have a favorite Jim Croce song?" or "Was 'Time in a Bottle' written for you?" I think about my husband Jim Croce, and smile at how he might have answered these questions.

Alternating between tales of Americana, portraits of crazy characters, and revelations of a very romantic autobiography, Jim Croce would have told you a "bigger than life" story in his down-to-earth way. He would have embellished his answers, making them personal because it felt good to share that common experience.

In concert, when humbly introducing his ballads or love songs, Jim would usually let the music speak for itself. But with his "story" songs, Jim's wit and charm exaggerated his heroes, making legends of "everymen" from lovers to operators, stock car boys to Roller Derby Queens.

"I use my storytelling in-between songs," Jim would say, *"to set them up, to make them broader in their appeal... so that people can say, 'Hey, I know that situation,' or 'Wow, I've seen that guy before.' When anybody sees someone with a pack of cigarettes rolled up in their t-shirt sleeve, they'll think of 'Rapid Roy the Stock Car Boy.' And that really makes me feel good, that my songs have given somebody something—a two-way exchange!"*

Jim's gift was his song, a sincere voice to sing it, and an insatiable enjoyment of sharing his talent. He knew in his heart it was what he was supposed to do, but still, he played every moment as if he were "playin' hooky."

In writing this book, I tried to keep my stories and the songs as chronologically correct as I could. But, while some of Jim's songs were spontaneous, others evolved over a longer period of time. Some came out of nowhere, others from Jim's musical history or his own or other's personal experiences gathered along the way. I want you to know that I really tried hard to be as accurate as I could. I read Jim's love letters again and again and found "unexpected in-between-the-lines messages." I studied notes, handwritten songs, listened to tapes, watched footage, and pored over scrapbooks, reviews, interviews and stories, too. So, all I can say is that in the end I've done my best. Jim, I hope I got it right!

Photographs and Memories
Written at our kitchen table in Lyndell, Pennsylvania, 1972

*"But we sure had a good time, when we started way back then.
Morning walks and bedroom talks, oh, how I loved you then."*

It was a snowy night two days before Christmas in 1963. I was auditioning with the Rum Runners; we were contestants in a folk music contest at radio station WDAS in Philadelphia. Close to the station's parking lot, our old clunker was stuck in the snow. For fear of being late, I jumped out to push our car while my band members, six husky military cadets, sat inside the sedan teasing and chiding me on.

After the automobile was liberated, I looked up and saw this handsome, curly-haired guy staring at me from inside his VW Beetle. At 16, I wanted so much to impress him by looking older and cooler than I was. Instead, I waved at him impulsively like a little kid wearing my mittens. He smiled back sweetly, waved and drove on.

Once inside the studio, as I stood before the microphone tuning my guitar, I looked up through the smoky glass window into the control booth. There he was again. That cute guy from the parking lot was the judge for the audition! He looked shy and sensitive, yet, at the same time I felt like he was undressing me with every glance.

Trying to impress my perceived critic, I improvised without informing my band and performed a new and unexpected opening to our pre-rehearsed folk song. I mimicked the words a capella to a Marilyn Monroe interpretation of a song from the movie *Some Like It Hot*. "You've heard of instant coffee, you've heard of instant tea, well, you just cast your little ol' eyes on little ol' instant me."

When I finished, though dumbfounded, my band picked up their instruments and joined me in our unrelated folk song, "The Midnight Special." Next we played "The Cruel War" and completed our audition with Pete Seeger's "Where Have All the Flowers Gone?"

When we finished, the cute judge smiled at me sheepishly and came into the studio to talk to us. Tripping over the microphone chord to reach me, he introduced himself. "I like your voice," he managed. "Maybe we could sing together sometime." That night we won the audition and our romance began. For a decade, Jim Croce and I built a lifetime of memories together, some of which he wrote about in "Photographs and Memories."

Vespers
Written by Jim and Ingrid Croce at our home in Media, Pennsylvania, 1969

*"She'd call me in the evenin' and ask me to come over,
She'd be standin' by the window, with her hair down around her shoulders,
We'd talk a while and then she'd smile, and then we'd close the door,
And she would sit beside me, and we would talk no more.*

*The bells would ring at six o'clock and she'd be in my arms,
Her head upon my shoulder gently resting,
And then she'd wake and look at me, not knowing I'd been watching,
Kiss me softly then drift off to sleep."*

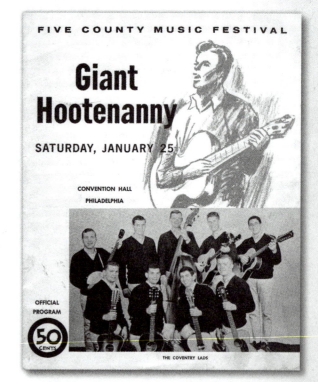

Tim Hauser of The Manhattan Transfer (top row, far left), Jim Croce (top row, far right), and Tommy West (bottom row, far left)

Two weeks later, at a hootenanny at Philadelphia's Convention Hall, Jim Croce sought me out and found me practicing my guitar. I had selected my dress carefully that night wanting to look hip and older than I was. I wore my tall black boots and a tight white sheath with black stripes running up the sides. Jim, in contrast, dressed conservatively in his collegiate, highly starched oxford shirt, navy blue v-neck sweater and light beige jeans with pressed creases. I was so happy to see him I could barely breathe.

But before I could even say hello, Jim planted his foot firmly in his mouth and bantered, "That's a nice dress you're wearing. You look like a little skunk!" Mortified by his comment, I withdrew and put down my guitar. Jim, realizing that he had hurt my feelings, moved closer and, with his candid humor, apologized and told me sweetly, "But you look really pretty, Ing."

Very politely, he asked if he could play me a song. I had never heard Jim Croce sing and had no idea of the treat I was in for. He tuned my guitar and sang me a haunting, traditional blues ballad called "Cotton-eyed Joe." I was mesmerized. His voice was so warm and sincere; it healed my wounds. That night my band won the contest, but it wasn't nearly as important as winning his heart. Jim and I both couldn't wait to see each other again.

"Vespers," which Jim and I wrote together for our 1969 Capitol Records album, reveals Jim, the troubadour, as the true romantic he was. When we met, he had an idealized dream of being a worthy lover of lost or imagined love. The song's title was chosen by Jim, referring to the sixth of seven separate canonical hours set aside for prayer in Catholicism. I think it aptly expresses his Catholic guilt, as well as his amorous desires.

You Don't Mess Around with Jim

Written at our kitchen table in Lyndell, Pennsylvania, 1972

"You Don't Mess Around with Jim" came out of the lifestyle and songs Jim Croce loved to hear and sing when he was growing up in Philadelphia. There was a lot of black music crossing over in the '50s and early '60s. With Jim's ability to learn a song after listening to it just once, he built a great repertoire of R&B and Rock and Roll songs through the years. As a young teenager who wanted to meet girls and who lived just blocks away from Dick Clark's *American Bandstand*, Jim figured if you didn't play varsity, you better play music. And though it wasn't until 1971 that this song was actually written, songs like *"Big Boy Pete" and *"Searchin'" by the Coasters were the impetus for "You Don't Mess Around with Jim" and "Bad, Bad Leroy Brown."

Jim, age 18

In 1961, as a freshman at Villanova, Jim Croce joined the glee club where he met Tommy (Picardo) West, who later became his producer. Jim and Tommy bonded over the music they played at school and in rock and roll bands on the road. Then, in 1963, when I first met Jim Croce, folk music had become the rage. He was a judge for a folk music contest in which the band I was singing with, the Rum Runners, had taken first place. Pete Seeger, the Weavers and Odetta were headliners for that night's concert. Jim also played as part of the Villanova folk group, the Coventry Lads. Then, after graduating from college, he got his own "hands-on" experience working around pool halls while selling radio airtime for a black radio station, WDAS in West Philadelphia.

Finally, in 1971 it all came together. Jim wrote this song at our kitchen table and sent it to Tommy West and Terry Cashman who produced *"You Don't Mess Around with Jim"* for Jim's first ABC Dunhill album. Ironically, when this song hit the charts in 1972, Jim Croce's first television appearance of "You Don't Mess Around with Jim" was on Dick Clark's *American Bandstand*, right around the corner from where Jim had grown up dreaming of performing on the show.

> "I remember a couple of things that really got me interested in the 'pool shark syndrome.' The English have that fancy billiard, and you walk around with a brandy glass and stuff like that. But the poolrooms over here are somethin' else. There used to be a place in Philadelphia that was an institution, called Allingers. I went up there one time to watch the best of the best, and they were gonna have one of these matches up there. It wasn't gonna be on TV; it was gonna be one of those underground things. There were these lights over the pool tables, and all these little bent people. 'Cause when you shoot a lotta pool ya know, you get a little bent. I said something to somebody, and somebody said something to me, and I said something back, and before I knew it I went down two flights of concrete steps, hitting the steel lips on my backbone, all the way to the subway. Ssshhheww! That sure put me 'into a world...' I mean that's a whole different world by itself, the world of pain. Some people get off on it, the warning system of the human body, and that's where I got to see the American phenomenon of 'pool cue justice.'" J.C.

* "Big Boy Pete" by Don 'Sugarcane' Harris and Dewey Terry; "Searchin'" by Jerry Leiber and Mike Stoller.

Mary Ann

Written by Jim and Ingrid Croce at our Bronx apartment, 1969

> "You'll know you're a man, when you meet Mary Ann,
> If you only hear the sound of her breathin'.
> She'll talk to you in words, in ways you've never heard,
> And you'll forget about the time when you should be leaving."

Jim's family home in Drexel Hill. Jim Croce, Diane Croce, Rich Croce and Ingrid Jacobson

A month after we met, on our third and most auspicious date, Jim picked me up in his dark green VW bug and took me for my first visit to the Croce family home. I was really nervous to meet Jim's mother Flora, "The Flower" as Jim jokingly called her. She had always been curt with me when I called to ask for Jim. But as soon as I entered the Croce's living room, smelled the roasted garlic and peppers, and saw the Fellini-esque array of aunts, uncles, nieces and nephews everywhere, I was intrigued.

Jim's favorite aunt, Ginger, welcomed me with a big hug. And next to her, dancing by himself to the voice of Tony Bennett on the Victrola was her husband, Uncle Sam, a savory Sicilian larger-than-life character4. He grabbed me from behind and swung me around by the waist, attempting to dance with me. Fortunately, Jim intercepted and took me into the kitchen to meet his mother. On the way he whispered in my ear, "Watch out for Uncle Sam, Ing. He's got a gun!" It was hard for me to tell when Jim was kidding.

Jim's brother Rich and his girlfriend Diane welcomed me into the kitchen. Jim's father, a tall, silver-haired, handsome man, came over and shook my hand warmly. "The Flower" was busy darting around the kitchen, preparing a Northern Italian feast. Though cordial, she did not seem particularly "happy" to meet me.

First of all, I was just 16, and I was Jewish, my parents had been divorced, and Flora got it right away that Jim and I were crazy about each other. This was not her plan, especially for the eldest son of a traditional Catholic-Italian family. Maybe worse than my history and traditions was the fact that I supported Jim's dream of becoming a professional musician. That was no way for her son to make a living! After all, Flora Croce believed that "the Beatles had ruined this world," and "the people in the music business were gypsies and thieves."

When Jim and I were writing this song, we had just rented our first New York apartment together, in the Bronx. We were passionately in love. Jim told me he was expressing the feelings he had for me in "Mary Ann."

I Am Who I Am
Written by Jim and Ingrid Croce, from my poem in 1964; recorded for our Capitol album, *Jim and Ingrid Croce*, 1969

Ingrid performing solo at The Main Point

When I met Jim, I was a high school sophomore, transforming from a 16 year-old cartwheeling cheerleader at Springfield High into a Joan Baez inspired folkie. I wanted to do it all: play music, make art, do gymnastics, study psychology, travel the world and find love.

Jim was four years older, a talented and mischievous Villanova sophomore. He had studied the Kama Sutra and was looking for "someone to be the recipient of his long anticipated glee." And Jim was always busy finding ways to get out of doing whatever it was he was supposed to do so he could play music and just be happy. During our "practices" we'd listen mainly to a lot of folk and country artists like Woody Guthrie, Gordon Lightfoot, Ian and Sylvia, Len Chandler, Merle Haggard, Simon and Garfunkel, Joan Baez, Bob Dylan, Johnny Cash, Jimmy Rodgers, Lefty Frizzell and many, many more. Music was our bond, and we wanted to write together.

Shortly after we met, I shared a poem with Jim that I had written at school. Jim put music to it on the spot and this was our first song together. We later recorded "I Am Who I Am" on our 1969 Capitol album, *Jim and Ingrid Croce*.

Child of Midnight
Started in 1966 at RISD and completed in the Bronx, 1970

After Jim and I had been singing together for a few weeks, he invited me to Villanova to perform with him as a duo for the first time in public. Before the concert, I met Jim's construction buddy, Billy Reid, and his wife Dee. Billy opened the show playing bluegrass banjo and Jim backed him on guitar. A trio played next, and then it was our turn to perform. We sang three songs in harmony; Jim sang one alone. The audience called us back for two encores. We did an Ian and Sylvia song, "Four Strong Winds," and ended with Phil Ochs' "Power and Glory."

To close the show, one of Jim's closest friends, Joe "Sal" Salvioulo, got up to sing the protest song, "Just a Little Rain," by the writer and social commentator Malvina Reynolds. Sal was a brilliant and flamboyant folklorist, a singer-songwriter who greatly engaged Jim's humor. I liked him right away.

After the show, Sal invited us back to a party at his apartment in Lansdale. He lived on the top floor of an old Victorian mansion. It was so cool and romantic. When we arrived, it was packed with friends and musicians, and Johnny Mathis' "Misty" was on the record player.

Joe Salvioulo, in the early '60s

Photo by Paul Wilson

Jim asked me to dance and led me onto the floor. I was so turned on at the thought of being close to him. For a moment our bodies were one; his arms were around me and it felt so right. But then, Jim stepped back and started doing this strange and unusual dance, churning his elbow and lifting his leg like a dog about to pee. Instantaneously, everyone's attention was drawn to Jim doing his "dog dance" in the center of the floor.

Though the spell was broken, I already thought he was the most adorable and funny guy I'd ever seen and I was so happy to be with him. But, when I looked around the room, I realized, for the first time, that I wasn't the only one who had strong feelings for Jim. There were at least four or five other girls who did, too. Some belonged to a musical group Jim had put together called the Haveners from Cabrini, a Catholic girls college near Villanova. They were all crazy about him. These college girls were staring me down, checking me out and looking me over as if I'd committed a sin.

Then another Johnny Mathis song began to play, "It's not for me to say, I love you." Jim danced me into a nearby bedroom, closed the door, and we sat down on the bed. He kissed me tenderly. I was a virgin, with a girdle under my tight, tight black skirt. While I was falling madly in love with Jim, I felt so young and inexperienced in those surroundings and compared to all those college girls. It was such an innocent time. We made out passionately, but Jim respected me, and we postponed our lovemaking for later.

Two years later, while I was away at Rhode Island School of Design, Jim would visit me for long weekends. We started "Child of Midnight" and "Mary Ann" and finally got to record these songs in 1970 when Jim and I lived in the Bronx. John Stockfish, who had been the bass player for Gordon Lightfoot was living and working with us that year, and his wonderful bass line punctuated the depth of feeling we had hoped to express.

> "Her lips said good bye but her body said stay
> I knew I should go, but I stayed anyway
> And they called her Child of Midnight..."

Ballad of Gunga Din
Written at his home in Drexel Hill, 1966

Jim reading selected poems by Leonard Cohen

When Jim started at Villanova University, folk music was gaining popularity. He was lucky to get a job doing a three-hour folk and blues show on Sundays interviewing guests like Mississippi John Hurt and Son House. Hearing their music reminded him of the songs he'd listened to while growing up. Jim's father loved traditional jazz and blues. The phonograph was seldom without a stack of Turk Murphy, Fats Waller, Bessie Smith, Eddie Lang or Joe Venuti records.

Jim was also into the humor of Will Rogers, Lenny Bruce, and totally turned on to the hipness of Lord Buckley ("The Nazz"). He enjoyed Haiku poetry, read Leonard Cohen, and learned all the bawdy ballads of Oscar Brand and the folk songs of Woody Guthrie, Leadbelly and Ramblin' Jack Elliot. They all became part of Jim's personality and performing style.

With a repertoire of over two thousand songs, from folksy blues, jazz, popular music, rock and roll, and even Elizabethan and bawdy ballads, Jim was building enough confidence to write his own music. As an avid reader of poetry, he decided to put music to Rudyard Kipling's poem "Gunga Din." When he played it for the first time at the Riddle Paddock for a bunch of rowdy drunk sheepherders from Australia, he got a standing ovation and even a tear or two, which encouraged Jim to keep writing. In 1966, on his first self-made album, *Facets*, Jim published his first songs "Gunga Din," "Sun Come Up" (co-written with his brother Rich) and "Texas Rodeo."

Alabama Rain
Written at our kitchen table in Lyndell, Pennsylvania, 1972

As boyfriend and girlfriend, Jim and I would spend a lot of time at each other's homes. I always looked forward to his mother's amazing Northern Italian home cooking and Jim loved talking philosophy and religion with my dad. Many nights, at our home, Jim would tutor me in history and geography. If we accomplished enough, as our treat, we'd park in the lot at the Baptist church down the street from my house. I was never very good at memorizing facts, but if I learned my lessons quickly, we'd climb into the back seat of Jim's VW bug and makeout until my ten o'clock curfew put an end to our fun.

When Jim wrote Alabama Rain for his second album Life and Times, he had been on the road performing just about every night, away from home for almost a year. Though the trappings of a musician's lifestyle were fun and intoxicating and Jim was enjoying his freedom, it was lonely. When he came home, he was immersed immediately in family life and reminisced about what it was like to be young and madly in love.

> *"We were only kids but then, I've never heard it said
> That kids can't fall in love and feel the same.
> I can still remember the first time I told you "I love you.""*

Jim and Ingrid with their VW Bug at the Croce Family Home in Drexel Hill, PA

Which Way Are You Goin'
Written by Jim and Ingrid Croce in the Bronx, late '60s

When Jim Croce was born on January 10, 1943, to Flora Babucci and James Albert Croce Sr., first generation Italian Americans, they wanted their son to have a good American upbringing, a college education, and a solid nine to five job with the promise of a pension. At the age of four, Jim started singing at Sunday family get-togethers and had a half hour repertoire of songs that included everything from Fats Waller's "Oyster in the Stew" to Guy Lombardo's "Boo Hoo." Jim began his formal training on the accordion. Immersed in music from an early age, his father proudly took his "Little Jimmy" to perform at St. Dorothy's Church's talent shows. A natural performer, Jimmy squeezed and fingered his little accordion, singing with confidence for the crowds.

Around the age of 16, while working a summer job at a toy store, Jim met two old black gentlemen who stocked the shelves and played guitar during their breaks. Jim asked for lessons. They agreed to teach him chords if he brought his own guitar. So Jim took his brother Rich's neglected clarinet down to a pawn shop on Race Street. He traded it in for an old Harmony F-slot guitar and started to play.

Jim's First Holy Communion

The next summer, Jim took a job as a contract painter at a hospital where he once fell two full stories on the job. Even though Jim was phobic and accident prone, he continued to paint, but with an alternate motive: Across the street he had made a friend of a construction foreman, Billy Reid, who played country and bluegrass guitar and banjo on lunch breaks. Billy was a larger than life character, and he and Jim traded songs and instruments, developing a close bond.

By the 1960s, "the times they were a changing." We were fearful of nuclear war, and our first Catholic president President John Fitzgerald Kennedy had just been assassinated. A lot of our friends were being shipped off to Vietnam. Blacks were still segregated, it was a crime to be gay, and women and minorities were still treated as second-class citizens. It was a tumultuous period, but a terrific time to be young and alive. We had a whole world of opportunity and new possibilities. Jim saw that professional musicians as diverse as Bob Dylan, the Beatles and Frank Sinatra were making a good living at playing music. I encouraged Jim to follow his dreams, but his family insisted he follow theirs. Never wanting to disappoint anyone, it was hard for Jim to find the words to tell his parents how he really felt. We wrote this song about the times we were in and for Jim; he hoped his feelings would get across to his mother and dad.

> "Which way are you goin', is it hard to see?
> Do you say what's wrong for him, is not wrong for me?
> You walk the streets of righteousness but you refuse to understand,
> You say you love the baby, but you crucify the man,
> You say you love the baby, but you crucify the man."

Pa (Song for Jim's Grandfather)

Written by Jim and Ingrid Croce in the Bronx, late '60s. Jim and I wrote this song as part of a group of about 20 songs we put together for a children's TV program in Boston. Ultimately, we lost the show to Hoagy Carmichael, but we still have the songs.

Jim's uncle, Massimo Babucci "Pa", Jim Croce, Pascal Croce (Jim's Paternal Grandfather)

Sometimes to socialize and for entertainment, we'd take Pa, Jim's maternal grandfather, to the Italian Club on Passyunk Avenue in Philadelphia. He'd play bocce with his cronies and we'd all dine together on the daily pastas, while "the regulars" smoked stinky stogies and got into heated conversations.

"Pa", Massimo Babucci, had moved into the Croce household when Jim's grandmother passed away. Having three generations living under one roof was difficult for Flora, but for Jim it was fun. He loved listening to Pa's stories in Italian about his time in the Carabiniere (Italian Police), about his job as a tailor at Botany 500, and of the little dog on the piazza in Abruzzi who liked to pee on the statues in the plaza. Pa's short-term memory was gone, but he had intricate details about his past. Later, as Jim approached his senior year at Villanova, Pa's stories about Italy inspired him to travel. He already spoke German and Italian and was tired of living in the suburbs under his parent's strict regulations. Family traditions required Jim to live at home until he married, so he found a way to get out from under their control.

Jim had heard about an opportunity through his university to tour Italy, the Middle East and Africa as part of a folk quartet. So he went downtown to Philadelphia with his guitars in hand to audition alongside hundreds of students from the East Coast. The Student Association was selecting a single student from each quadrant of the United States to be a goodwill ambassador for the tour. In addition to musicianship, the students needed to speak a couple languages, have good knowledge of American Politics, and possess the social skills to communicate them. When Jim won, he called excitedly to tell me he was at the doctor, getting his shots and leaving right away.

"The American Folk Quartet."
Jim travelled with Gene Uphoff from Minnesota (guitar, banjo, auto harp, recorder); Susie Levin (Mamma Cass) from California (singer, guitar); and Southerner Bob Knott, Jim's closest friend on tour (guitar, banjo, harmonica, kazoo, mouth bone).

Walkin' Back to Georgia
Written at our kitchen table in Lyndell, Pennsylvania

When Jim returned from his tour abroad, he grasped the true power of song as an international language and was more determined than ever to make music his profession. "When we couldn't speak the language," Jim recalled, "the music got across all the barriers. We ate just what the people ate, except I remember having a little trouble downing a cooked calf's foot once."

While Jim was abroad, the president of the company where his father worked wrote a piece about Jim's travels in their Armstrong Associated Steam Company newsletter. *"If Jim Senior needs a new hat size, we are not surprised or can we blame him... Jim Junior is now a senior studying psychology at Villanova University. We certainly hope that Jim the folk singer follows in his father's footsteps. His psychology degree and inherited talents should make him a crackerjack salesman of traps and humidifiers."*

It was hard for Jim to break away from the confines of his family's traditions. He was a good son, but he felt a growing discontent with the life he was expected to lead, especially after his trip abroad, and he was feeling smothered.

He wrote me often while he was away. When he returned, our relationship suffered. I didn't understand the "disconnect" and I was heartbroken. But to avoid feeling rejected and insecure, I threw myself into my school work and decided to study art and psychology. When I got accepted to Rhode Island School of Design and Brown University that spring, I moved to Providence, Rhode Island.

As soon as I left, Jim's love letters and tapes started coming every day. He'd tell me how much he loved me, how sorry he was to have hurt me, and how he had gone to see a jeweler in South Philadelphia to learn about diamonds so he could buy me the perfect ring.

The idea for the song "Walkin' Back to Georgia" was started around this time. Ray Charles had recorded "Georgia on My Mind," a 1930's Hoagy Carmichael hit. And like Hoagy, Jim just liked the sound of the word Georgia. He finished the tune for his first LP on ABC Dunhill in 1972 with the following words:

> "She's the girl who said she loved me,
> On that hot Georgia Macon Road,
> And if she's still around, I'm gonna settle down,
> With that hot lovin' Georgia girl."

Portrait of Jim taken at Moore College of Art in 1967

Big Wheel
Written at our home in Media, Pennsylvania

While I was still away at school, Jim had a gig four nights a week at the Riddle Paddock and occasionally at private parties. On his nights off, he'd visit his old friend and construction foreman, Billy Reid, and his wife Dee. They played bluegrass, ragtime and country music on the front porch of Billy's farm outside Coatesville. Bill had the persona of a "Big Jim Walker," "Rapid Roy" and "Speedball Tucker" all wrapped up in one and his influence on Jim was undeniable.

Billy Reid was a good friend and knew Jim needed money, so he graciously got him a job at Sweeney's driving a dump truck and hauling rocks and dirt off the construction sites. He got Jim a union card and, best of all, he introduced Jim to his "salt of the earth" buddies: Reds Mullen and Emil Cianfrani. "Big Wheel," "What Do People Do," and later, "You Don't Mess Around with Jim," "Speedball Tucker," "Rapid Roy," "Careful Man" and "Singin' the Blues" were all rooted in Jim's experiences with these rowdy, colorful characters who did construction and drove trucks for a living.

from left: Reds Mullen, Jim Croce and Emil Cianfrani at Sweeny's Truck yard

"Big Wheel" is a simple trucker saga from our first Capitol record, *Jim and Ingrid Croce*. But, it paved the way for Jim's continued blue-collar and country approach to music. Jim originally played these songs on his Gibson 12-string, but after listening to a lot of Joan Baez and Chet Atkins he began learning to fingerpick. Unfortunately, this was just about the time he busted his right index finger with a sledgehammer while on the job. Undaunted, Jim worked in various country bars and developed a picking technique that would ultimately include his thumb and three fingers, and he turned to a 6-string guitar. In 2002, our son A.J. and I released the *Jim Croce Home Recordings Americana* CD. The songs had been taped on a trusty Wollensak recorder my father gave us as a wedding gift. Every time I hear the songs, they connect me to the front-porch music we played in the country back then, and it's just like Jim is there and Billy's right beside him.

These Dreams
Written at our home in the countryside of Pennsylvania, 1972

In December, Jim came to visit me at The Rhode Island School of Design and asked me to marry him. I was 18 years old when he picked me up in his soft top '61 VW bug and drove me to the sand dunes in Wellfleet for our first romantic weekend together.

On a windy winter's night in our little room in Cape Cod, Jim played a song he had written just for me called, "Ingrid." The song, which has never been released, has a melody that is ironically the forerunner to "Time in a Bottle." It was my engagement gift. He placed a diamond ring on my finger, which he had proudly saved for by working construction, selling radio airtime and playing in the bars at night.

Ingrid at RISD in 1965

From the moment I met Jim I knew I wanted to be with him for the rest of my life. But I was so young and it seemed to me, though it was unconventional at the time, that we should live together first. I could be his woman, and then his wife. But Jim was insistent and adamant that we get engaged right away. He was convinced that his family would disown him if we moved in together before we wed. So, that weekend we became officially engaged. In April 1966, after our engagement party, Jim's mom and dad gave Jim the opportunity to make an album, as our engagement gift. They hoped that if Jim completed this project he would be finished with his childhood dream of becoming a musician and get a "real job."

The earnings from record sales were ours to keep as a further wedding gift. It was their way of helping us get started in our own home. Only 500 copies of the album he called *Facets* were originally produced. But when they sold out over night, Jim got a glimpse at the prospect that he might actually be able to become a professional musician. Contrary to his parent's hopes, the album *Facets* was a success and reinforced Jim's passion for music. After that, Jim never wanted to do anything else.

Jim and Ingrid performing at The Riddle Paddock in 1967

On August 26, 1966, Jim and I were married on a wooden bridge over a small stream in my family's back yard. A couple years before we married, my father had bought the wonderful home on Dogwood Lane in Wallingford, Pennsylvania from Dick Clark of *American Bandstand* fame. It was just family at our wedding, and the home's backyard was the perfect setting. Later, Jim wrote these words, perhaps remembering our wonderful times together:

> "Once, we were lovers, but somehow things have changed;
> Now we're just lonely people, trying to forget each other's names.
> What came between us, maybe we were just too young to know.
> But now and then I feel the same,
> And sometimes at night I think I hear you calling my name,
> Mm mm mm, these dreams,
> They keep me goin' these days."

Operator (That's Not the Way It Feels)
This story was born at the PX in Fort Jackson, South Carolina; matured at the Riddle Paddock; and completed at our home in Lyndell, Pennsylvania

Jim and Ingrid when Jim returned from Fort Jackson, SC

Once we got married, Jim and I couldn't wait to move in together. But our five day honeymoon ended with a teary-eyed kiss goodbye at Penn Station; Jim got his head shaved, his boots polished and left for the Army National Guard. Since joining two years earlier, Jim had been waiting anxiously to do his basic training. Then, just as we were about to be wed, they summoned him to Fort Jackson, South Carolina to satisfy the Guard's requirement. He wanted to be in communications...so they made him a lineman.

Jim wrote me the most wonderful love letters every day, and sometimes twice a day. He also wrote about his strong distaste for authority, which led to the necessity to take basic training twice. But as always, Jim's discontent fueled his humor and even at boot camp found his wit and musical talent could be used in his favor.

Jim practiced his guitar and entertained his fellow soldiers whenever he could. Once they heard Jim's music, his superiors (who had yelled and screamed at him and called him "maggot") soon asked him to perform for them at the Officers Club. Of course, every chance Jim had to get out of work, he took it. It was at Fort Jackson that Jim really started to get a lot of new ideas for his songs.

"I got the idea for writing "Operator" by standing outside the PX, waiting to use one of the outdoor phones. There wasn't a phone booth. It was just stuck up on the side of the building, and there were about 200 guys in each line waiting to make a phone call back home to see if their "Dear John" letter was true. And with their raincoats over their heads, covering the telephone and everything, it really seemed surreal that so many people were going through the same experience, going through the same kind of change, and to see it happen especially on something like a telephone, talking to a long distance operator—just registered...

When I got out of the army, I was working at a bar where there was a telephone directly behind where I was playing. I couldn't help being disturbed by it all the time, and I noticed that the same kinda thing was happening: people checkin' up on somebody or finding out what was goin' on, but always talkin' to the operator. And I decided I would write a song about it." J.C.

Bad, Bad Leroy Brown

This song began at Fort Dix and was completed at our home in Lyndell, Pennsylvania, 1971

Over the last 25 years, 30 to 40 guys have come into Croce's Restaurant & Jazz Bar in San Diego, claiming to be the authentic Leroy Brown. Who's to say who's the real "Leroy Brown," but what I do know is that the real story began back in December 1966. My father became very ill. Before he passed away, Jim was able to get a transfer for "hardship" leave from Fort Jackson, South Carolina to Fort Dix, New Jersey.

"Leroy Brown is somebody I met in the United States Army, down in Fort Dix where I had an MOS of being a Field Communications crewman, which is a wire man. That's a big long name for "target." I was climbing these poles and running this wire and it was a great experience: I've used it often in my daily life.

But Leroy was stationed down there at Fort Dix, and about a week after we got there we were sittin' around talkin' and one night he said he didn't like it there anymore and he was gonna go home. So he did. He went AWOL. Came back at the end of the month to get his pay, which was kind of a mistake. But when he got out of the stockade it was a lot of fun to just sit down and talk, because he had opened up. It was like an enlightening experience for him. And, after gettin' out of the cage, Leroy just turned into a completely different person. I mean, he's probably doing books today or somethin', giving lectures on some corner. I used to just listen to him talk and to see how 'bad' he was. I knew someday I was gonna write a song about him..." J.C.

Jim in uniform at Fort Dix, 1966

Rapid Roy (The Stock Car Boy)

Started at 12 West Front Street, our home in Media, Pennsylvania, and finished at our kitchen table in Lyndell, 1971

In December, after my father died, Jim's obligation with the National Guard was over. He still had to go to local meetings at the Armory so I was lucky to score this great 200 year old, three story brick house, across from the Media courthouse for only $100 a month, not far from the Armory.

For my junior year, I continued to take the train to school. Jim took the car to work when he got his one and only shot at an office gig, working at radio station WHAT in Philadelphia. *"I was writing those jive commercials for a black R&B station. And I was doin' 'em once in a while, too. 'Get yo'self a boss drain,' that's a raincoat. I still have a whole street vocabulary. I didn't sell much time, but I sure learned a lot. I'd be up on Germantown Avenue trying to sell air time to a jazz bar and as the only white person up there they thought I was a cop or a collection man."* So that job didn't last long.

In the meantime, Jim still attended his National Guard meetings regularly and developed a good friendship with Ronnie Miller, who introduced Jim to a whole new slice of life. On Sundays, we'd head out to the stock car races where Jim filled his head with all the details of the racers, the crowd and the moment, capturing a portrait of all the colorful characters in "Rapid Roy (The Stock Car Boy)."

Jim and Ingrid in front of their home in Media, PA.
Photo from the archives of "The Philadelphia Inquirer" story, August 13, 1967

"He's too much to believe,
You know he's always got an extra pack of cigarettes, rolled up in his t-shirt sleeve.
He's got a tattoo on his arm that says, 'Baby.' He's got another one that just says, 'Hey,'
And every Sunday afternoon he is a dirt tack demon in his '57 Chevrolet."

Workin' at the Car Wash Blues

This "blue-collar anthem" was written at our kitchen table in Lyndell, Pennsylvania and completed on the road

In 1967, after Jim returned from Fort Dix and left his gig at WHAT, he took a substitute position at Pulaski Junior High, teaching Special Education. *"I've still got scars on my hands from the knife wounds,"* Jim said. *"I was the seventh teacher since that September...What a year. I got beat up by an eighth grade girl who weighed about 280 pounds in seventh grade. It was a dangerous place."* It was no wonder Jim left at the end of the year, but it is a wonder that he lasted as long as he did.

While some of the kids were real sweethearts, and Jim really helped them learn things, others were scary. They'd be slashing our tires and bashing in our car, which we ultimately spraypainted brown because of all the dents and affectionately named "the raisin." Jim once said, *"My job was essentially to teach these eighth and ninth grade kids to read. So I'd tape songs by the Supremes and the Drifters, then we'd study the lyrics as I played the tunes on the guitar. They loved it and we were really getting somewhere, but it was a little too unorthodox for the administration."*

Jim at Pulaski Jr. High with his students

Four nights a week we played for our supper and 25 bucks at a funky club called the Riddle Paddock in Lima, Pennsylvania, where Jim had performed when I was away at RISD. We'd practice our new songs for the boisterous crowds, consoled by their great response and still believing that someday Jim would make music his career. After Jim completed a hellish year teaching Special Education, we both got jobs as instructors in art and music at "The Lighthouse" summer camp to make ends meet. In the fall of 1968, Jim went back to driving a truck at the quarry. I opened "The Hundred Little Pot Shop" in the front room of our house to sell my paintings and pottery and help pay my tuition for Moore College of Art, where I had transferred from RISD so I could attend school in Philadelphia. During this "character development period," Jim was the cook in our family. He'd pick me up from the train station after school and every night he'd serve me the most amazing Italian suppers. He tried making his own dandelion wine, too, which was not quite as successful. He used to joke on stage about it and about Ripple, "the only wine in the States that's never seen a grape." These times inspired Jim to write one of my favorite Croce tunes ever, "Workin' at the Car Wash Blues."

> *"Well, all I can do is to shake my head, you might not believe that it's true,*
> *But workin' at this indoor Niagara Fall, is an undiscovered Howard Hughes,*
> *So, baby, don't 'spect to see me, with no double martini in those high-brow society news,*
> *'Cause I got them steadily depressin', low-down mind messin', workin' at the car wash blues."*

What Do People Do

Written by Jim and Ingrid Croce in Media, Pennsylvania for our college concert circuit tour 1969-70; recorded for the *Jim and Ingrid Croce* album, 1969

"I wrote a lot of country stuff, but there is one elementary law to be considered here," Jim said. *"You can't come from South Philly and be a true country singer. There's no way. It wouldn't be in character."*

In the summer of 1969, Jim and I went to Mexico. I had won an art fellowship to study pottery and painting at San Miguel de Allende. When we returned home for my senior year at college, Jim was really sad. He wrote, *"We stop being what we are when we stop doing what we do."* And Jim was tired of just making a living. While his charm and intelligence could have landed him work anywhere, **his heart was set on a profession in music, everything else was just a job.**

Jim and Ingrid in New York City
photo by Nick Venet

A few weeks after school started, Tommy West called Jim and told him to come up to New York City and give the "music business" a try. Tommy, an old college buddy, was now a record producer and familiar with the music Jim and I performed at local bars and coffee houses. As much as we wanted the opportunity, I still had to finish college and we were just barely able to pay the bills. But, when we got a deal with Capitol Records, I felt this was Jim's chance. Tommy encouraged us to come up to New York City, promising plenty of studio work and assuring us if we weren't happy, I could go back to school the following year.

We moved into an apartment on the Upper East Side of New York City with Tommy and his first wife, Pat. After signing contracts, we went into the studio to record our first album, co-produced by Cashman, Pistilli and West, and the famous Nik Venet. Nik produced artists like Bobby Darin, the Beach Boys and Linda Ronstadt, and he was a great collector of Indian artifacts, an artist and photographer. He took the photos of Jim and me for our first album, *Jim and Ingrid Croce*.

While the record was being "sweetened" and "mixed" in the studio, Jim and I had to leave to promote the album on the college concert circuit. We travelled over 100,000 miles that year, living on good ol' American blue plate specials at colorful truck stops and cafés. We stayed in small motels and in private homes of the people from the colleges who had invited us to play. These were our happiest times. Jim and I were young, broke and so much in love. We weren't dismayed by the modest gigs or the roadside cuisine we suffered as long as we were making music and doing it together. I often drove so Jim could play guitar and we could write songs along the way. We listened to country music and the Grand Ole Opry on the radio. We were happy that our song "What Do People Do" went over so well in Kentucky and Tennessee. It gave us hope that our album would sell.

Hey Tomorrow
Written by Jim and Ingrid Croce in the Bronx, 1970

By the close of the '60s, we were experiencing firsthand that America was in great turmoil. Racism was tearing the country apart and activists were busy with anti-war demonstrations. While Jim and I were performing as a duo on the college concert circuit, we got caught in the middle of riots in the cities and on college campuses where students were closing down student unions and striking against the war in Vietnam.

The excitement we had experienced promoting our Capitol album, *Jim and Ingrid Croce,* was over. Jim grew disillusioned with the "music business." We had no money to pay for gas and his frustration only increased when he finally heard our album for the first time. It was not at all what Jim had expected.

"We did an album and I couldn't understand why it became a trade secret. They ground it up and made Grand Funk records out of it," Jim would say, with small malice and a big grin. *"It sold six copies in PX's in Thailand. We were playing these small colleges, a thousand miles apart, working them for a week, have one day off and driving a thousand miles to the next one, sometimes a 24-hour drive, getting there exhausted, just in time to play."*

After a year on the road, we returned to a tiny rented apartment in a big, dirty old building in the Bronx. It was awful. It even had bars on the windows so you wouldn't jump out! Without any gigs or money, there we remained, cooped up, practicing and writing every day, patiently waiting for our careers to take a turn for the best. It was then that we met John Stockfish. He had played bass for Gordon Lightfoot, one of our favorite singer-songwriters. John was an amazing musician. He liked our music and needed a place to stay. So, Jim invited him to move in with us for a while. John brought his bass and his wife; they stayed for six months. These were cramped and tense times, but Stockfish helped us refine our act and recorded with us, too. By the summer of 1970, Jim and I had written over 20 original American folk songs for a children's show we were hoping to do in Boston. When we were ready to present our music to the producers, we sadly discovered that Hoagy Carmichael had gotten the job. And we wrote "Hey Tomorrow."

Jim and Ingrid in Gramercy Park, New York City

> *"Hey tomorrow, where are you goin'? Do you have some room for me?*
> *Night is fallin' and the dawn is callin', I'll have a new day if she'll have me."*

"Hey Tomorrow" and several of the songs we wrote in the Bronx, along with cuts from our Capitol album and some unreleased sides, have been re-mastered for the *Jim Croce Anthology 50th Anniversary* CD: "Spin, Spin, Spin"; "Vespers"; "Big Wheel"; "And I Remember Her"; "Cottonmouth River"; "More Than That Tomorrow"; "Migrant Worker"; "Child of Midnight"; "Stone Walls"; "King's Song"; "Walkin' Back to Georgia"; and "Age."

Box Number 10
Started in the Bronx in 1970 and completed in Lyndell PA, 1971

Jim and Ingrid in the Bronx, NY

After losing our chance to do the children's show, the failure of the album, the year on the college concert circuit, and then coming home without a penny to pay the rent, we were at the end of our rope. Jim got a couple of calls from Tommy to play a few jingles in the studio. Without gas money, he would ride his bike through Harlem and Central Park to the downtown studio to sing some "oohs and ahhs" as a backup singer, just waiting for the chance to actually sing some words. By this time we had no idea how we were ever going to make a living playing music. I wanted to encourage Jim, but the truth was we had left home and moved to New York City to begin our careers. It just felt like it wasn't our time.

Worst of all, Jim now had to face his parents and admit they were right. The words to the song "Box #10" are not only Jim's story, they resonate with so many people who come to the city and lose their way.

> *"Well, I was gonna be a great success, things sure ended up a mess,*
> *And in the process I got messed up, too.*
> *Hello, Mama and Dad, I had to call collect, 'cause I ain't got a cent to my name,*
> *Well, I'm sleepin' in the hotel doorway, and tonight they say it's gonna rain,*
> *So if you'd only send me some money, I'll be back on my feet again,*
> *Send it in care of the Sunday Mission, Box #10."*

New York's Not My Home

Conceived in NYC and completed at our kitchen table in Lyndell, after what felt like the end of Jim's music career

Jim and Ingrid in Upstate New York, 1969

Jim hated to disappoint anyone. But once he apologetically told his buddy and producer, Tommy West, that he had given it his best shot, he was ready to go home.

With his adrenaline pumping, he carried our air conditioner, which never worked, down 17 flights of stairs. Attempting to vent his anger, he threw it like a weapon on the landlord's front step. Sadly, he missed, and with his toe throbbing, his back aching and all our possessions piled high on the truck, he performed his final act of defeat. He heaved his bicycle up on top of our pile of belongings only to have it reverse direction and plummet down. The spokes of a wheel caught his ear. Blood was coagulating on Jim's ear and tears of pain were welling up in his big brown eyes as we drove away in the rental truck with our old red Saab in tow. Without enough money to pay the New Jersey toll, I threw a handful of pennies in the basket and Jim drove like a bat out of hell across the border. We felt like fugitives in our own land. Once we reached the Howard Johnson's on the other side of the bridge, I looked behind at the imposing skyline. It was majestic all right, but it never felt like home!

Age

Written by Jim and Ingrid Croce at our home in Media, Pennsylvania, 1968; originally on our Capitol Record, *Jim and Ingrid Croce* and was also included in Jim's final album, *I Got a Name*

In some ways, the song "Age" was intuitive. After our experience in the "music business" and Jim losing a trusted friend along the way, the song rang truer than ever.

> "I traded love for pennies, sold my soul for less,
> Lost my ideals in that long tunnel of time.
> I turned inside out and round about and back again.
> I found myself right back where I started again."

After the demise of our Capitol album and the difficult experience of living broke in NYC, we had no idea where our music careers were headed. What we did know was the cost of our souls wasn't worth whatever the business had to offer. So, in October 1970, escaping to the countryside, we found a new home in Lyndell, PA. Naively, we thought we were finally free.

But soon after we settled in, Jim started getting intimidating phone calls and threats about our music business contracts. It went something like, "No matter where you go or what you write, it belongs to us forever, in perpetuity!"

Being earnest and poor, we were confused. Our "attorney," who also represented our publishers, our manager and our record company, was definitely not on our side. When we signed, we weren't given a copy of our contracts so we asked a friend of a friend, a Philadelphia lawyer, for help. Sadly, we didn't have the money to pay for legal advice, and Jim didn't want any conflict with his old friend, so we just hung out in the country and wrote songs for ourselves.

Then a really good thing happened during our rural retreat. We became best friends with the amazing guitarist and singer-songwriter Maury Muehleisen, who we'd met at our apartment in the Bronx through our old friend Joe Salvioulo. This was during Jim's "lying low" period and it was perfect timing. Maury had just made an album on Capitol Records with Tommy West and Terry Cashman. Jim backed Maury up and helped him promote his songs at local clubs and college concerts, too. When Maury's album, *Gingerbread,* failed to bring him the success he truly deserved, the young prodigy moved in with us in Lyndell. While living together, the three of us enjoyed a close, personal and musical friendship, and there was a feeling of great optimism.

Jim at our kitchen table in Media, PA

> "Now I'm in my second circle and I'm headin' for the top.
> I've learned a lot of things along the way.
> I'll be careful when I'm climbing, 'cause it hurts a lot to drop,
> And when you're down, nobody gives a damn anyway."

Tomorrow's Gonna Be a Brighter Day
Started in Lyndell when we were getting back to the earth and could actually see the stars and feel the morning dew

This was a throwback to the folk, blues and traditional songs Jim played me when we first met, like "Cotton-eyed Joe" and "Seven Golden Daffodils."

Once we were on the farm, things started to mellow. We had our own garden by the kitchen door and joined a food co-op in Chester County. Melvin Goldfield, an artist and dear friend who lived nearby, had us over to his geodesic dome to check out his artwork. And every week Jim would go down to South Philly in Melvin's truck to pick up the produce from the farmer's market and stop nearby for truck parts. Once, when they drove by the Tinicum Swamp, they stopped at an old junk yard near where Melvin grew up and met up with a raging canine protecting his junk. The term "meaner than a junkyard dog" was coined there and became legend in Jim's song, "Bad, Bad Leroy Brown."

Jim really loved having company over to our home. It was a party all the time. I would be busy baking bread and serving meals in between making music and taking turns practicing new songs. Jim, Bill Reid and Gene Pistilli would tell stories of one-upmanship until they were so outrageous someone would just start singing another song. And whether it was Tim Hauser, Pat Rosalia or Erin Dickens from Manhattan Transfer; Arlo Guthrie; James Taylor; or Bonnie Raitt returning from a gig at The Main Point, people just stopped by.

Jim and Ingrid in Lyndell, PA

On rare occasions when there were just two of us in the house, Jim's perfect morning meant waking up early and brewing a pot of strong espresso, sitting down at the kitchen table with a couple of good books, a pad of paper, a tape recorder and his 6- and 12-string guitars.

An hour or so later, when I was still asleep in our cozy bed, Jim would wake me gently with a traditional demitasse cup of thick, black Italian coffee topped with a lemon zest and a kiss. This "wake-up call" from my best friend meant he wanted to make love or we had guests that needed my "attention," or that he just wanted to make love.

> "I'm sorry for the things that I told you, but words only go so far.
> And if I had my way, I would reach into heaven and I'd pull you down a star, for a present...
> And I'd make you a chain out of diamonds and pearls from a summer sea.
> But all I can give you is a kiss in the mornin' and a sweet apology."

Roller Derby Queen
Written at our home in Lyndell, 1972

Our little place in the country became the "Original Croce's Restaurant" with hippies, Hell's Angels, intellectuals, priests, farmers, teachers and pretty young things that liked to come by and listen to Jim and Maury sing. Of course, Billy Reid would come by, too. And Jim got work playing at the local bar on an occasional Saturday afternoon, where he met the original "Roller Derby Queen."

Bill Reid in Lyndell, PA

"Now this is a tender, touching bar room love song that took me about five years to write because I couldn't find the right words. I was playing in a bar one Saturday afternoon and I noticed this beautiful little lady, about that high, kinda chubby. And my rule of thumb is... at 350 pounds you're a person, at 400 you become a place. Well, she was hangin' in there, and I noticed right after I'd gotten finished singin' 'Okie from Muskogee,' that she was clappin' real hard and this part under her arm was shakin' back and forth. And I got really excited.

So I went over and talked to her and even with her sittin' on a stool with that bleach blond hair piled up that high, four or five cans of spray net on it so you could tap on it and it would make sounds. Great lady, it looked like one of those hats that you see a drum majorette wear, or the Pope. Now the Pope he's got a hat, he's got that ultimate hat. But she had a hairdo that looked just like that. The only thing she was missing was the great big message ring where he can send things in code. 'Pope to Cardinal, Pope to Cardinal.'

But I wanted to really write a song about this lady, because I fell in love... and I start talkin' to her and I asked her if I could buy her a drink, and she said, 'Su-ure'... and I bought her a shot and a beer. Back home we call 'em boilermakers, that's just a straight shot of whiskey and a bottle of beer. The little one makes the fire and the big one puts it out. And they're just such a great drink if you like to fall down.

But I found out she used to be in a roller derby and she was from Texas, and I thought, man I just had to write a song about this lady. And then her husband comes in... now, he was a State Trooper..." J.C.

Time in a Bottle
Written at our table in Lyndell, Pennsylvania, 1971

I remember when I told Jim we were going to have a baby. The look on his face was a combination of fear and ecstasy. Though Jim always wanted a family, his big, sad, brown eyes registered, "Oh, my God, more responsibility!" Push had finally come to shove and it was now or never. This was his chance to make it in the music business, or it would be a nine-to-five job forever.

"When I found out we were gonna have a baby, I decided I was going to put every bit of energy I had into getting back to music. And I felt very strong about the things I was writing."

That night Jim sat down at our little kitchen table and recorded the haunting melody and words for "Time in a Bottle." Maybe it was a premonition that he wouldn't be around long or maybe he was just afraid that there wouldn't be enough time to make things happen the way he wanted to for our baby and me. Whatever it was, Jim got really serious about his music and focused on writing for a new album. He was using descending lines in his songs like Maury had played on piano and guitar. The music was more complex and the songs more honest.

Jim greatly respected Maury's talent and appreciated the beauty and restraint of his lead guitar. In performance and in person, Jim and Maury were both growing. Maury shared his classical training and amazing musical talent, Jim his natural skills at performing and his down-to-earth way of relating to his audience. When Maury and Jim played "Time in a Bottle" and "Operator," there was a new depth and dimension to their music and to their friendship.

Jim, Ingrid and Adrian James visiting brother Rich in Florida, 1967

Jim and A.J.

In February 1971, still afraid to record because he didn't understand our contractual agreements, Jim set aside his personal regrets about his friendship with Tommy West and sent him a cassette of a half dozen songs with a note that said, *"I just wrote these songs and I'd really appreciate just anything you could do with them. Get them recorded by someone else. Things are kinda tough."* The tape contained the songs "Operator (That's Not the Way It Feels)," "Walkin' Back to Georgia," "You Don't Mess Around with Jim" and "Time in a Bottle." Tommy listened to the new songs and had Jim and Maury come up to New York to discuss recording another album.

On September 28, 1971, almost a month later than planned, Jim helped me bring our son Adrian James Croce into the world. He spent a couple of weeks home with us, and then he was off to record *You Don't Mess Around with Jim*, his solo debut album on ABC Dunhill, at the Record Plant in New York City. Soon after its release in May 1972, the album yielded Jim's first Top 10 hit—"You Don't Mess Around with Jim."

Jim at home in Lyndell, PA

Hard Time Losin' Man

Written at our home in Lyndell; 1971; included on Jim's first solo LP, *You Don't Mess Around with Jim*

Jim on the road

"Hard Time Losin' Man" told a story that all folks who have ever seen hard times could relate to. It certainly was true to life for us. While we were waiting for A.J. to be born, we had a series of broken down trucks and cars. We were truly sweating whether any of them would get us to the hospital in time. In an interview, Jim later told this true story:

"I got caught on the expressway one night and this Philadelphia cop who looked at the registration discovered it was two years out of date. Then he discovered it was registration for another car. Then he discovered that my driver's license had expired and, top of that, the car was falling apart. He thought about all this for a few minutes and then apparently concluded that what he'd seen could not possibly have occurred. It must have been a mirage. He just told me just get off the expressway before you get caught."

"Oh, I saved up all my money, I'm gonna buy me a fancy car;
So I go downtown to see the man, and he's smokin' on a big cigar.
Well, he must have thought I was Rockefeller, or an uptown man of wealth.
He said 'boy I got a car that's made for you, and it's cleaner than the Board of Health'
Then I get on the highway, I'm feelin' fine, I hit a bump.
Then I found I bought a car held together by wire, and a couple a' hunks of twine.
And you think you've seen trouble, well, you're lookin' at the man, hmm, hmm.
Who's the world's own original hard luck story, and a Hard Time Losin' Man."

Speedball Tucker

Written at our kitchen table in Lyndell, Pennsylvania

"When you're down is when you get the ultimate sense of justice. That's the kind of thing I always enjoyed about driving a truck. You'd be workin' around people that really knew what they were doin'."

Jim stored stories in his head about all the characters he met along the way and when it was time, he wrote songs about them that were just about two and a half minutes long. His Haiku poetry, which he read and wrote often, helped him to condense his thoughts into few words. While playing live, just before Jim would sing "Speedball Tucker" and Maury would make the sound of the stock car speeding around track, Jim would tell this story about his truck drivin' days.

Our old Chevy Truck with 3 matching wheels

"This was another part of my character development. I got both my thumbs bent back the other way because y'know they've got these big steering wheels, great big things that when you hit a hole while you're turnin' the wheel, your thumb is going to be taped up for a couple of days or a couple of weeks. So, anytime you see these guys drivin' these big rigs, they've always got their thumbs taped up. And they're pretty happy, too, because on the long hauls you have to get into tryin' to stay awake a little longer, to make the haul profitable. And so you can get stuff there on time.

So, the truckers, a lot of these guys go into these truck stops which are like pharmacies on the road. Ya stop there to get all those things that the guy in the commercial tries to sell to the kids in the school yard. I've met a couple of guys that have had maybe six or seven thousand 'West Coast Turn-Arounds' under their seat in a brown paper sack. Now I don't take 'em... I just like having them around, in case I need 'em."

Careful Man

Written around our kitchen table in the country; recorded for Jim's second ABC album *Life and Times*

Jim had all kinds of sayings he coined during his lifetime. A couple of his favorites were: *"What's good for the sick is better for the well,"* and *"If you dig it, do it; and if you dig it a lot, do it twice."* In "Careful Man" Jim had fun with his tongue-in-cheek humor. He was writing good songs all the time now, playing his music, and travelling at warp speed, storing up those "West Coast Turn-Arounds," just in case he needed 'em.

> *"I don't drink much, I don't smoke, I don't be hardly messin' round with no dope,*
>
> *Yeah, I used to be a problem but now I am a careful man.*
>
> *Stayin' up late, havin' fun, done shot up every single shot in my gun,*
>
> *Yeah, I used to be a lover, but now I am an older man. Yeah, I used to be a lover, but now I am a careful man."*

Jim with his 6 string Ovation, 1973

Got No Business Singing the Blues

Written at our home in Lyndell for the *Life and Times* album, 1972

> *"It's all a matter of attitude," Jim laughed. "I've put a lot of miles on my truck checkin' out attitudes, and it looks to me like the best one is to be easy, take what comes, and have a good time."*
>
> **Jack Haffercamp-Chicago Daily News, Saturday-Sunday, September 22-23, 1973.**

Jim liked to be happy. It was his nature to find humor in just about everything. Growing up in Philadelphia just miles from where Dick Clark's *American Bandstand* was recorded, Jim was definitely influenced by certain groups that really knocked him out, like Fats Domino, the Coasters and the Impressions.

"The things the Coasters used to do, their visual act was something I could always get into. It was something you could see around the neighborhood, too. It was real. There weren't any heavy messages in the delivery and the subject matter. It was just 'stomp your feet, get up and have a good time, dance, laugh and forget yourself.' It wasn't the morbid 'ain't it terrible' school of songwriting. Not all music has to be so heavy. I went through that 'tell-the-world-how-to-live' stage, but I feel that's all been said. Sure, a lot of my songs are message songs, but basically I believe music is to have a good time with." J.C.

Ingrid Croce, late '60s

(Next Time), This Time
One Less Set of Footsteps
Both written at our home in Coatesville, 1972

Jim and Maury in Amsterdam with the ABC Dunhill promotion team

Although Jim had become more serious about his music, he never wanted to get too serious. He would leave that up to me. He was just glad that I could take care of business and found great humor in the fact that I was working so hard doing it. After being away and on the road for long spans of time, it was hard to come home. And if things got "intense," he could flip on a dime. These songs are about the other side of that coin.

This was a tough time for us and we knew a lot of people who had experienced relationships that went wrong. In the songs "(Next Time), This Time" and "One Less Set of Footsteps," Jim tapped into human emotions that were universal. I think a lot of us have felt this way when we've been sad, angry and blaming the world for the trouble we're in.

But Jim's favorite line from one of his favorite tunes was Fats Waller singing: "You're not the only oyster in the stew." That's how Jim really connected to the world. He knew we were all in it together.

"I find that you can get a bunch of people from different backgrounds into one room for a concert and they will get off on it when you present the basic experiences that are common to us all."

Five Short Minutes
Written on the road, 1972

Following his song "Five Short Minutes," Jim hedged, at a concert..."*That's part fantasy,*" he said flashing his ever-present grin. "*I have to be careful about that one. I really do...but the funny thing about not being in a rock and roll band is that we don't get the full blast of that groupie scene that is alleged to be out there. I've been playin' music about twelve years now, and I've seen a lot of parties. I've seen the sweet young things with their black fingernail polish and stars on their cheeks, but most of the time I just go back to the hotel, work on some songs and go to bed alone.*"

Jim and Maury in their dressing room before a show

After Jim Croce's first two albums were released, and "You Don't Mess Around with Jim," "Time in a Bottle" and "Bad, Bad Leroy Brown" hit the music charts, Corb Donahue played some of Jim's music to a new ABC Dunhill artist named Jimmy Buffet. Jim and Jimmy first met in L.A., then down in Florida, and later, wherever they could on the road. They had a lot in common; their love of music, good stories and their appreciation for women bonded them like fraternity brothers on the road. Jim had just written "Five Short Minutes," in honor of his groupies and Buffet's "Why Don't We Get Drunk and Screw," which was one of Jim's favorite Buffet tunes at the time.

Recently
Written at our farmhouse in Lyndell and on the road, 1972

Jim and A.J. in Lyndell, PA

"Jim's greatest grace as a human being," said ABC Dunhill executive and personal friend Corb Donahue, "was that he viewed his stardom with an amused distance. He was like a bystander watching it happen to someone else."

In 1973, Jim's second album topped the charts and he came home to relax and spend some time together with A.J. and me. Needless to say, I was a little more than surprised when I saw an entire film crew trucking up our driveway the day after he returned! There were about 15 people descending upon our house, unannounced to me, to record a promotional video of "Jim Croce at home on the farm." It was to be used to promote Jim's performances for college concerts. Jim knew I wanted some family time alone, so he had conveniently forgotten to tell me about the crew, hoping to avoid confrontation and my disappointment. Once they arrived to our home, it was time to make my famous muffins and pick squash and herbs from our garden. Jim headed down the road to the general store called Frank's Folly for some eggs, thick slab of bacon, a few six-packs of beer and Frank's local chatter.

Soon, my best friend, Judy Coffin, Maury Muehleisen's girlfriend, showed up with some beautiful, strange or funny things to add to our bounty along with her young sons Andy, Jake and Ed. I squeezed fresh orange juice, prepared vegetable frittatas, grilled buttermilk pancakes, and ground the beans for freshly brewed coffee and espresso with lemon zest. The crew all stayed for lunch, and dinner, too, and then Jim generously invited them back again the next day for more.

*"Used to be that I could see a reason to be happy 'cause I was free,
But then recently it seems I've been letting your memory get to me."*

Dreamin' Again

Written at our farm in Pennsylvania, 1972; included on Jim's last LP, *I Got a Name*

Looking back, I'm glad Jim "conveniently" forgot to tell me about the filming. Rick Trow and his crew captured my favorite footage that day and I cherish it again and again. Best of all, sharing those few days around our kitchen table with new friends renewed us. We were just a happy family having fun on the farm again.

Jim once said, *"Ingrid understands what this is all about, and isn't back home thinking I'm having the time of my life on the road while she's stuck at home with the baby. She's been on the road and she knows the grind."*

> *"Don't you know I had a dream last night, and you were here with me*
>
> *Lyin' by my side so soft and warm. And I dreamed you'd thought it over, I dreamed that you were comin' home,*
>
> *But when I woke up, Ah, my dream, it was gone*
>
> *I had been dreamin' dreamin' again, I had been dreamin' dreamin' again."*

Jim and Ingrid in Lyndell, PA, 1971

I'll Have to Say I Love You in a Song

Written at our kitchen table at the farm in Pennsylvania

Jim and A.J. at breakfast

Probably the two things that bugged Jim Croce more than anything were when people were confrontational or "grumpy." I'd been guilty of both. I wanted to just let things go, I really did. But it was so hard being apart. Then, when Jim came home, it was so hard, at first, being together. I wanted to be his support system but I needed his support, too.

After the film crew left, I asked Jim about our finances. We were barely making ends meet but Jim wouldn't talk about it. He hated questions as much as he hated confrontation. He just stormed out of our bedroom and went down to the kitchen table to brood. The next morning he woke me gently to sing me his new song.

> *"Every time I tried to tell you, the words just came out wrong, So I'll have to say I love you, in a song."*

Top Hat Bar and Grille
Started in San Diego and finished on the road

By now, Jim was playing big concerts and amphitheaters for thousands. He was opening for Woody Allen, George Carlin, Loggins and Messina, and Randy Newman. But his favorite gigs were still at the small bars and clubs where he got to meet people, ground level and face to face. One weekend Jim had a gig at the Funky Quarters, a small club where he really liked to play. Jim took me to San Diego and the minute I got there I knew why he felt so at home: It was laid back. The beaches and piers were like the postcards of California we'd grown up with on the East Coast. Best of all, the people seemed really nice, more relaxed and down to earth than the ones I'd met in L.A.

The Funky Quarters was the impetus for the song "Top Hat Bar and Grille." The characters Jim met there were like the folks he knew back home. We both felt like we belonged. Years later, I named an R&B music club next to Croce's after Jim's song. All kinds of people performed there, from Willie Nelson and Arlo Guthrie to Robin Williams and the Alabama Blind Boys. It was a great tribute to live music and I can surely picture Jim playin' there now!

Jim and Maury performing at Paul's Mall in Boston, MA

"It was more than just writing and recording. I was so into the live playing experience, which was probably a carryover from the folk times. It's so important— not just for feedback, but for feedout." J.C.

Lover's Cross
Started in L.A., continued in our hotel room in Mission Bay, and finished on the road

Jim, Ingrid and A.J. visiting the Croce's home, 1973

Once we decided to move to San Diego, I came out to California with A.J. to join Jim and find a place to live. We all stayed at a hotel on Mission Bay. By then I was pregnant for the second time and six and a half months along. Jim was having difficulty wrapping his head around the responsibility of yet another child. He had only been home occasionally during Adrian's first two years and he felt guilty, angry and exhausted from the road. Even more so, Jim felt like a failure. With no money to show for all his hard work and his time away, though he hated to admit it, he was standing at a crossroad and it was time to make some choices.

Jim was absolutely crazy about his little boy and he wanted to find a way to be at home with him and have his career, too. He wanted it all. *"I think Adrian James is havin' a lot of fun,"* Jim said. *"He's growing up around a lot of music. He has his own ukulele which he picks up and plays whenever he sees me."*

He also told reporters, *"Sure the touring is tough, but it's not like I'm some 17 year old away from home for the first time. I've been married a while now; I've got a son over a year and a half old. The days I'm out, I call them on the phone every night. We figure that for the time being, it's worth it."*
The National Observer, April 7, 1973.

It Doesn't Have to Be That Way
Written at our Lyndell home in the country, 1972

Jim was on tour in Europe when something terrible happened. I was alone on the farm with A.J. All of a sudden I was in terrible pain. It was too early for the baby to come. By the time I delivered our son, at the hospital, we lost him. Max died in childbirth while Jim was still on the road, and there was nothing either of us could do.

In August, 1973, A.J. and I moved to San Diego to set up our home while Jim was on the road. In September, Jim came home unannounced, wanting to surprise me. His arms were teeming with presents and his heart was filled with regret. He was anxious to make things right again, as if he knew there wasn't much time. He walked in the front door, kissed me and said, "I'm guilty," while wearing this big "shit eating" grin on his face. "It won't happen again," and he handed me an "S," his term for a surprise, like he always did whenever he came home. This time it was a Japanese pottery book that Cheech Marin had suggested I might enjoy. He had ordered me a potter's wheel, too. He said he wanted me to teach him to do ceramics and throw pots. Jim promised that the "Rock and Roll Craziness" was over, vowed to be faithful. He pleaded for forgiveness and joked that whatever I'd thought he'd done on the road wasn't half as much fun as I'd imagined. I told him, "I doubt that!" but he only grinned more.

That visit, we walked and talked on the beach with A.J. Jim was open about his deep concerns about the music business and the people in it. He was weary from the road and recognized the changes he wanted and needed to make. He sang A.J. to sleep every night, and said he wanted to be there to watch him grow up. Jim was doing his best to find his way home. It had been a hard road, but he believed, "It doesn't have to be that way."

Jim in Pennsylvania countryside, 1972

> "But it doesn't have to be that way, what we had should never have ended,
> And I'll be stopping by today, 'cause we could easily get it together tonight, it's only right."

The Hard Way Every Time
Written at our home in Lyndell

"Driving a truck kind of put me through enough changes and let me meet enough people that I had to decide the hard way if I wanted to stay in music." J.C.

> "But in looking back at faces I've been, I would sure be the first one to say,
> When I look at myself today, I wouldn't have done it any other way."

Jim performing

Once *You Don't Mess Around with Jim* topped the charts at number one, Jim started getting a whole lot of recognition, not only in the industry, but in the streets, too. By now, he was a real star, and there was hardly anywhere he could go that someone didn't recognize his face or his name. As grateful as he was for the acceptance of his music, Jim was rather shy about being famous. When we were out together, he avoided crowds and conspicuous places, opting for unpopulated beaches or just staying home.

Though Jim's music was at the top of the charts, his pockets were still empty. So, when he came home to San Diego one weekend, we went down to a thrift store in Ocean Beach to re-outfit Jim for the road. Roaming the aisles of used jeans, the stoned store clerk walked up clumsily to help Jim find stuff. When he got a good look at him, his eyes bugged out. "Hey, man, you look just like Jim Croce, man. You could make a lot of money pretendin' to be him, man." "Do ya think so?" Jim queried, and walked on shyly with a pair of used jeans and a Levi jacket in his hand, heading toward the counter. After paying for the Levi's with his last dollar, Jim was about to exit the store, when the salesperson stopped Jim again. "Hey man, I mean it. You look just like Jim Croce. He must be some kinda millionaire or something. You should try it, man." We weren't aware of any millions. Fact is we were livin' on small potatoes, and deeply in the red.

> "I just look at myself to find, I learn the hard way every time."

I Got a Name

"Alternating between tales of Americana, portraits of crazy characters, and revelations of a very romantic autobiography, Jim Croce would have told you a "bigger than life" story in his down-to-earth way." I.C.

Jim and Maury on a private plane

The weekend before Jim Croce left on his final tour, Jim and I made a dinner date. We had just moved to California and were anxious to be together and explore our new hometown. Unfortunately, back in 1973, the Gaslamp Quarter in downtown San Diego reminded us of Bob Dylan's "Desolation Row" with empty storefronts, sailors, tattoo parlors and ladies of the night.

We searched endlessly to find a good place to eat. Still hungry, we ended up at the historic Keating Building with no prospects in sight. Jim joked that we should just open up a restaurant and bar right there, on the corner of Fifth Avenue and F Street. We envisioned it as a place like our home in the country, where we would welcome folks to join us for dinner and wine, and play music all night long. That was one of the best weekends Jim and I had shared for a long, long time. After a dozen years of dreaming that he could make music his profession, it seemed things were finally going our way. Jim's songs were on the top of the charts. He was scheduled to host "The Johnny Carson Show" and was excited about doing a movie with Cheech and Chong.

When Jim left that weekend on tour, we were both really happy. We couldn't wait to celebrate Adrian James' second birthday party the following weekend. Four days later, Thursday evening, September 20, 1973, Jim called, as always, to let me know he was leaving for his next show in Sherman, Texas. With only a couple more concerts to go, he was finally coming home. Jim's last words to me on the phone that night were, "…I love you, Ing… Say goodnight to my little man."

An hour later, the plane that was chartered for Jim's make-up tour crashed on take-off from Natchitoches, Louisiana, killing everyone on board.

Shortly before Jim had left on tour, he completed his third album with the song "I Got a Name" by Charlie Fox and Norman Gimbel. It was a unique studio performance. Unlike others, it was performed without his guitar in hand. As a result, Jim's voice sounded strong but vulnerable. He remarked that while he hadn't written the song, he felt really close to it because his dad had recently passed away and he was now responsible to carry on his name.

After Jim's funeral, when I heard "I Got a Name" over the radio, I couldn't stop crying. I couldn't listen to this song without feeling Jim's presence and his absence all at the same time.

Fast forward a long 12 years to 1985. I opened a small café and catering business in Hillcrest and had just received notice from my landlord that my "month to month" lease was over. Serendipitously, a friend called to say she knew of an "open storefront" in the Gaslamp Quarter. When I got downtown, I realized I was standing on the very same corner where Jim and I had joked about opening a restaurant. I knew it was meant to be and that I should call it "Croce's Restaurant & Jazz Bar" as a tribute to Jim.

For over a quarter century, Croce's has been my way of keeping Jim's music and memory alive. I hope you will join us someday for our delicious American contemporary cuisine, nightly live music and a true Croce experience.

For more about Jim Croce, please join us at www.jimcroce.com

JIM CROCE
"in his own words"

"I find that you can get a bunch of people from different backgrounds into one room for a concert and they will get off on it when you present the basic experiences which are common to us all." **(1972)**

"Rather than picking a theme and writing about it, which I'd more or less done before, I became a song writer, writing from experience—character sketches, things like that." **(1971)**

"Top 40 chart success means that now I can do what I want to do, like take my masters in folklore at the University of Pennsylvania. It's an unusal feeling to be number one, especially for acoustic music. I don't seem to have suffered from the usual Top 40 stigmata, because each success has been a different type of song. And, we've been appealing to different age groups." **(Aug. 11, 1973)**

"Music is a form of recreation, an art form. It's a lot of things, but it shouldn't bring anyone down. I think music should make people sit back and want to touch each other."

"Music used to be primitive, now there are a lot of toys to play with in the studio, and a lot of artists are being produced out of existence. They're making records and sounds that are 'unproducible' on the stage."

"Not all music has to be so heavy. I went through that 'tell-the-world-how-to-live' stage but I feel that's all been said. Sure, a lot of my songs are message songs but basically I believe music is to have a good time with." **(1973)**

"I get very emotional about it to think that many people have enjoyed my work. But I don't think in chart terms when I'm writing. I think more in terms of feeling." **(1972)**

"I don't turn into something else when the spotlights go on. I'm the same then, as I am now talking to you. Getting into it at this age, there's a lot of stuff I'm not concerned about ego-wise. I just want to play music and relax a little bit once in a while." **(1973)**

"It was more than just writing and recording. I was so into the live playing experience, which was probably a carryover from the folk times. It's so important, not just for feedback but for feedout."

"I really think a lot of the old definitions and pillars are starting to fade. People are getting into just enjoying things. That's why the kind of music I write isn't directed at social documentaries, protests, anything like that." **(1972)**

"There's definitely an acoustic wave coming back. Acoustic guitar is an instrument you can take with you. There are not many rock bands that can just play. If you have a guitar, you can walk into a field and play or do it in your hotel room, you don't have to have amplification, special equipment." **(1971)**

"We're doing a very realistic, acoustic set of contemporary music, just playing acoustic guitars. I think there's an element about tradition that I like. I really think the attitude has an awful lot to do with it. Wanting to get out and communicate with people. Not just put on an act." **(August 19, 1973)**

"Chart tastes change. So I write songs as I feel them." **(1972)**

AGE

Words and Music by JIM CROCE
and INGRID CROCE

© 1969 (Renewed 1997) TIME IN A BOTTLE PUBLISHING, CROCE PUBLISHING and DENJAC MUSIC CO.
All Rights for TIME IN A BOTTLE PUBLISHING and CROCE PUBLISHING Controlled and Administered by EMI APRIL MUSIC INC.
All Rights Reserved   International Copyright Secured   Used by Permission

ALABAMA RAIN

Words and Music by
JIM CROCE

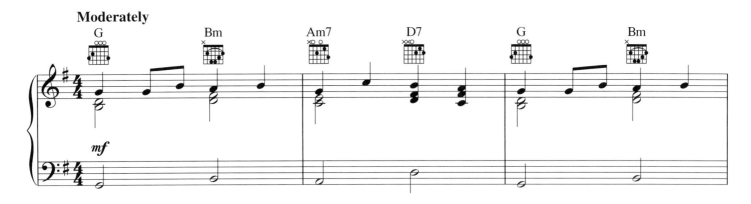

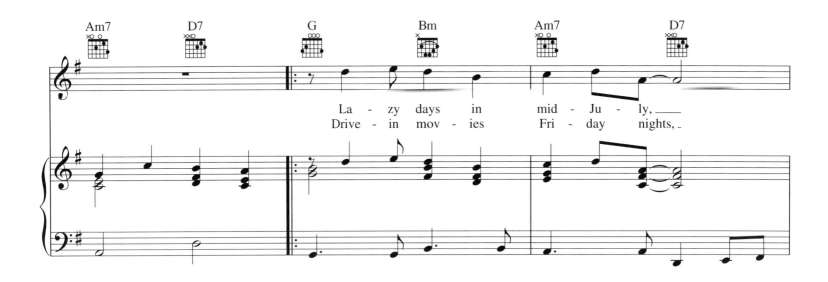

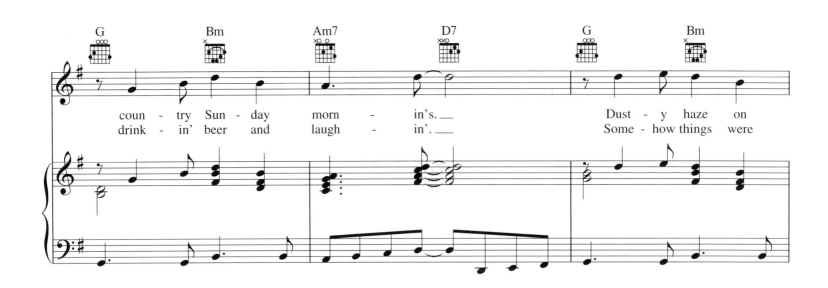

© 1972 (Renewed 2000) TIME IN A BOTTLE PUBLISHING and CROCE PUBLISHING
All Rights Controlled and Administered by EMI APRIL MUSIC INC.
All Rights Reserved   International Copyright Secured   Used by Permission

BALLAD OF GUNGA DIN

Traditional
Arranged by JIM CROCE

© 1966 (Renewed 1994) TIME IN A BOTTLE PUBLISHING and CROCE PUBLISHING
All Rights Controlled and Administered by EMI APRIL MUSIC INC.
All Rights Reserved   International Copyright Secured   Used by Permission

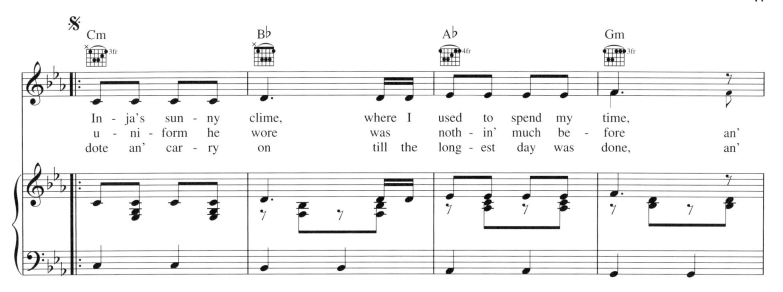
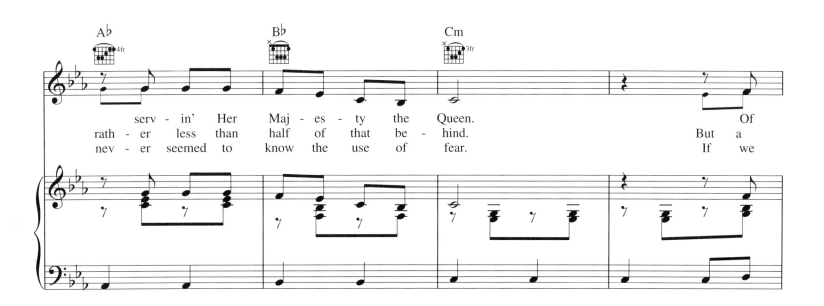
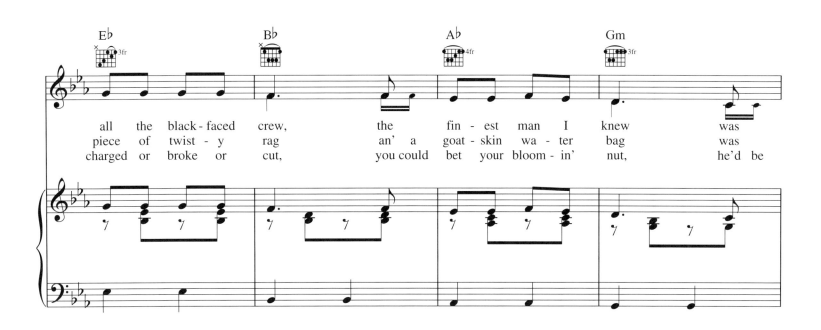

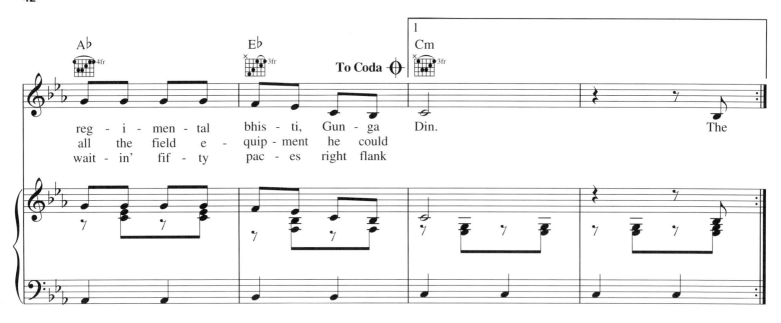

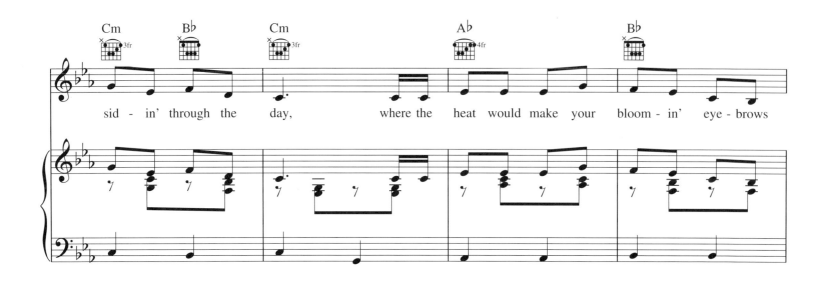

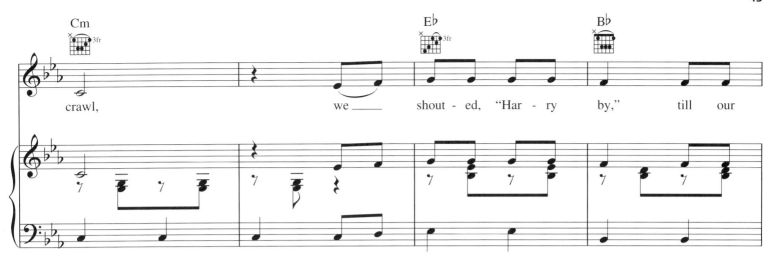
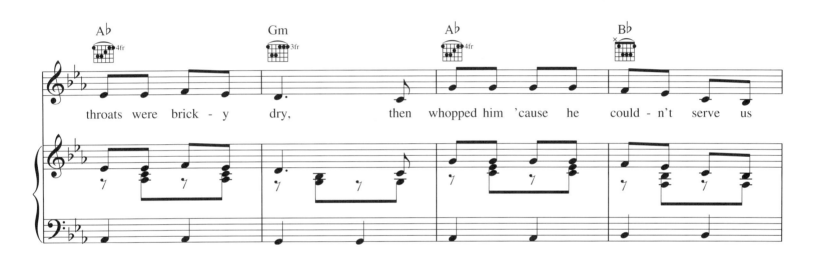
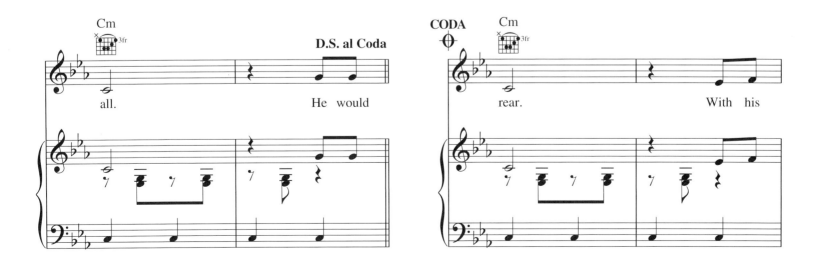

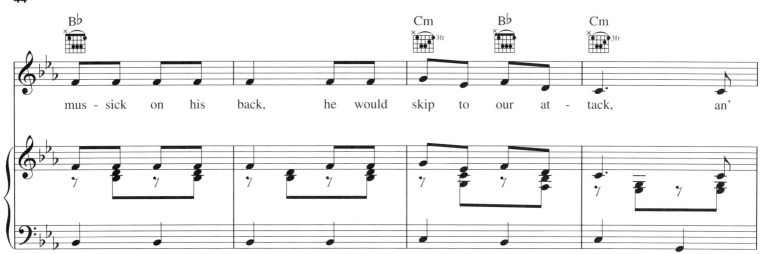
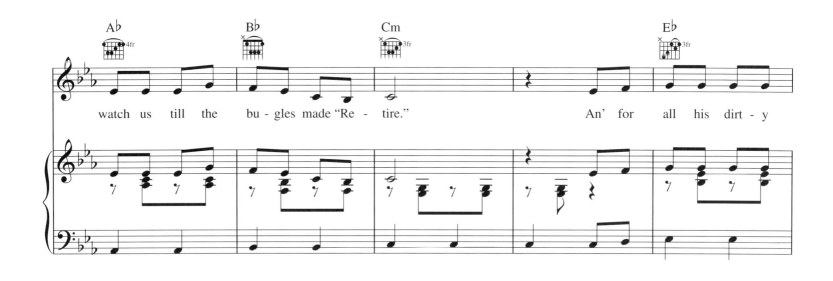

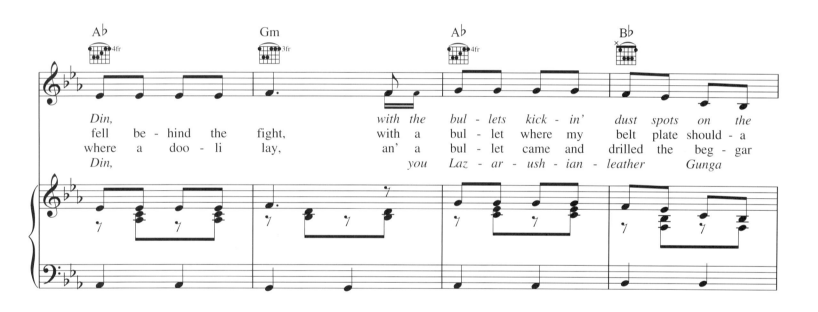

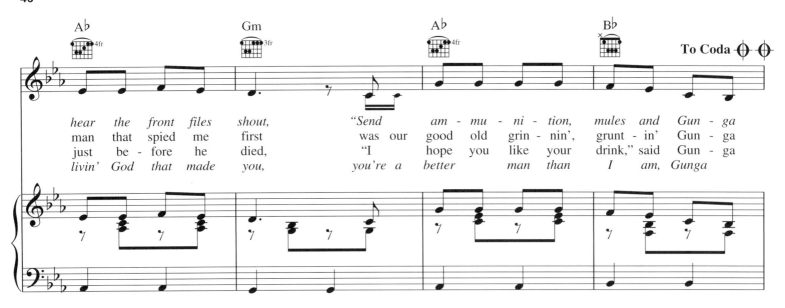
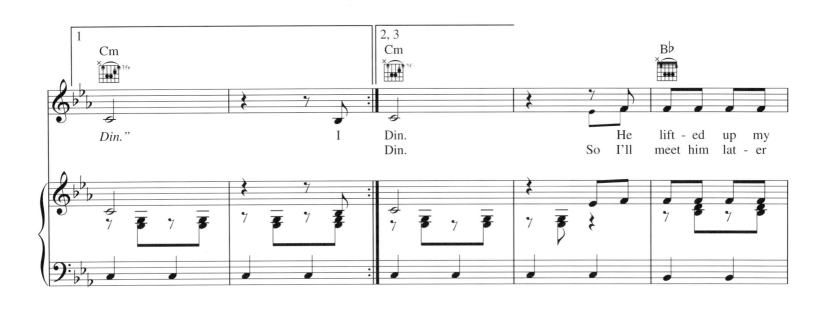

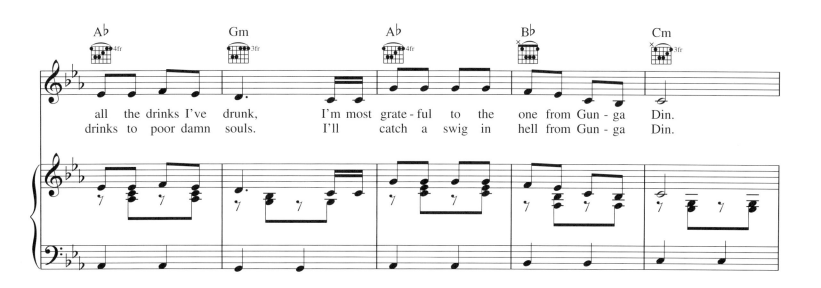
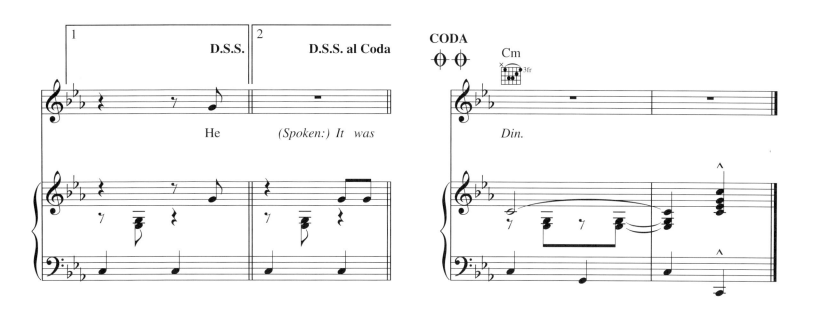

BIG WHEEL

Words and Music by
JIM CROCE

BOX NUMBER 10

Words and Music by
JIM CROCE

CAREFUL MAN

Words and Music by
JIM CROCE

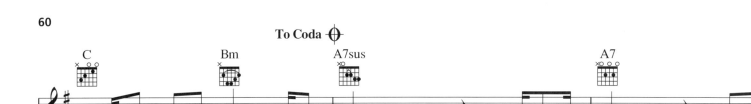

FIVE SHORT MINUTES

Words and Music by
JIM CROCE

Additional Lyrics

2. Oh, I saved up all my money
   I gonna buy me a flashy car;
   So I go downtown to see the man,
   And he smokin' on a big cigar.
   Well, he must'a thought I was Rockefeller,
   Or an uptown man of wealth;
   He said, "Boy, I got the car that's made for you,
   And it's cleaner than the Board of Health."
   Then I got on the highway, oh I feelin' fine,
   I hit a bump
   Then I found I bought a car held together by wire
   And a couple a' hunks of twine.

3. Oh, Friday night, feelin' right
   I head out on the street;
   Standin' in the doorway
   Was a dealer known as Pete.
   Well, he sold me a dime of some super fine
   Dynamite from Mexico;
   I spent all that night
   Just tryin' to get right
   On an ounce of oregano.

I AM WHO I AM

Words and Music by JIM CROCE
and INGRID CROCE

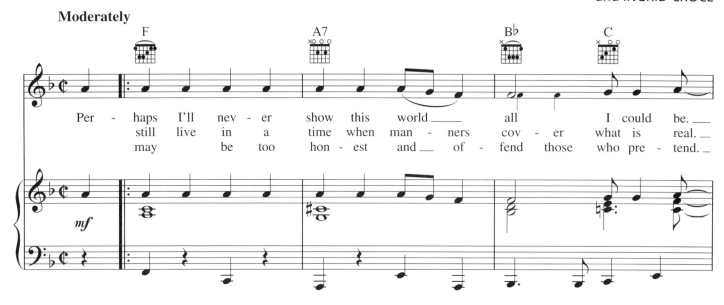

© 1969 (Renewed 1997) TIME IN A BOTTLE PUBLISHING, CROCE PUBLISHING and DENJAC MUSIC CO.
All Rights for TIME IN A BOTTLE PUBLISHING and CROCE PUBLISHING Controlled and Administered by EMI APRIL MUSIC INC.
All Rights Reserved International Copyright Secured Used by Permission

I'LL HAVE TO SAY I LOVE YOU IN A SONG

Words and Music by
JIM CROCE

© 1973 (Renewed 2001) TIME IN A BOTTLE PUBLISHING and CROCE PUBLISHING
All Rights Controlled and Administered by EMI APRIL MUSIC INC.
All Rights Reserved   International Copyright Secured   Used by Permission

I GOT A NAME

Words by NORMAN GIMBEL
Music by CHARLES FOX

© 1973 (Renewed) WARNER-TAMERLANE PUBLISHING CORP.
All Rights Reserved   Used by Permission

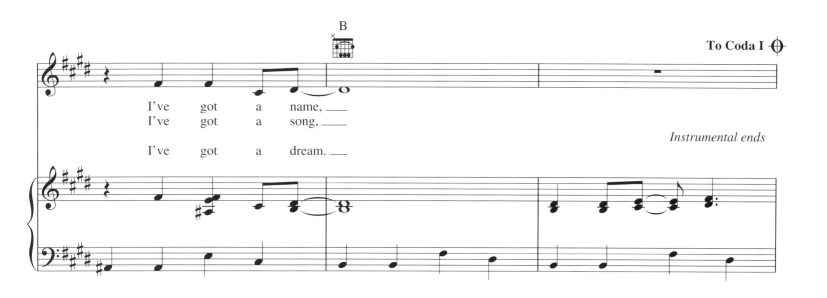

IT DOESN'T HAVE TO BE THAT WAY

Words and Music by
JIM CROCE

NEW YORK'S NOT MY HOME

Words and Music by
JIM CROCE

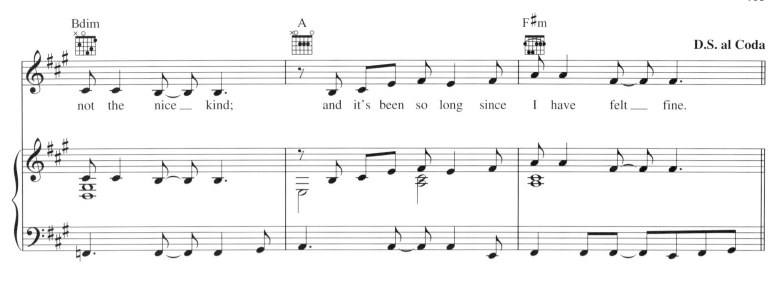
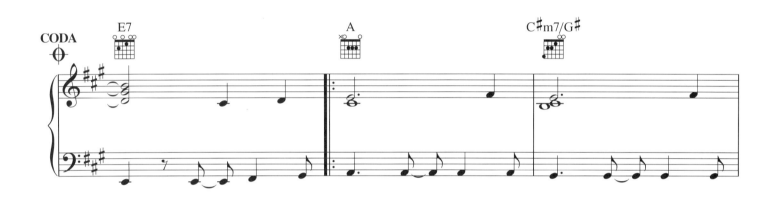
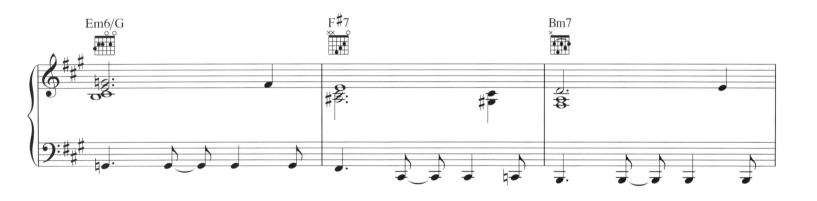
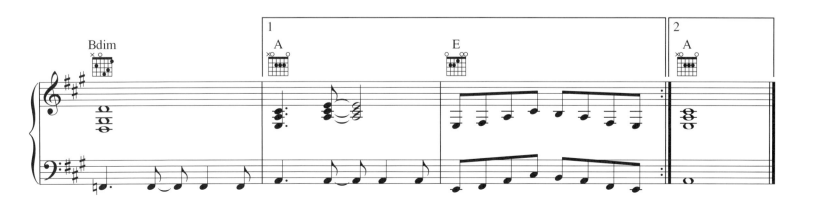

PA

Words and Music by JIM CROCE
and INGRID CROCE

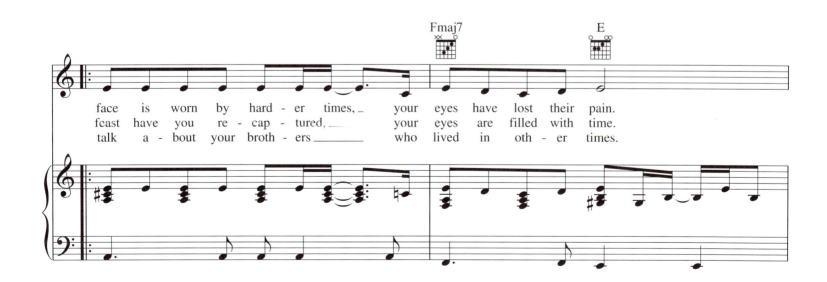

Your face is worn by harder times, your eyes have lost their pain.
feast have you re-cap-tured, your eyes are filled with time.
talk a-bout your broth-ers who lived in oth-er times.

© 1980, 2004 TIME IN A BOTTLE PUBLISHING and CROCE PUBLISHING
All Rights Controlled and Administered by EMI APRIL MUSIC INC.
All Rights Reserved International Copyright Secured Used by Permission

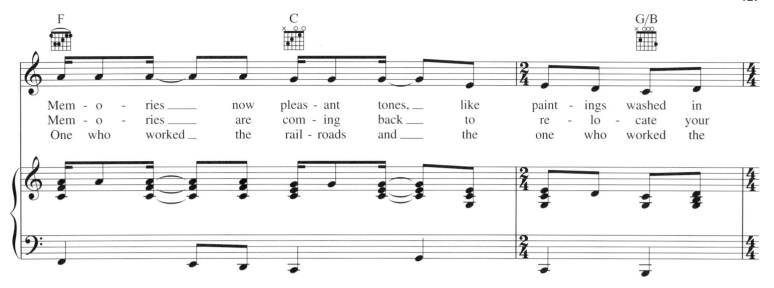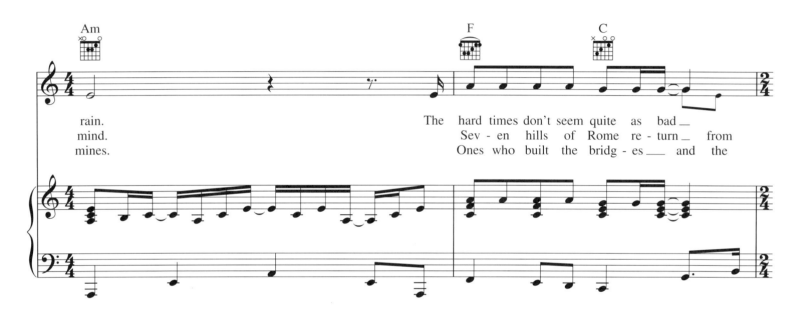

RAPID ROY
(The Stock Car Boy)

Words and Music by
JIM CROCE

ROLLER DERBY QUEEN

Words and Music by
JIM CROCE

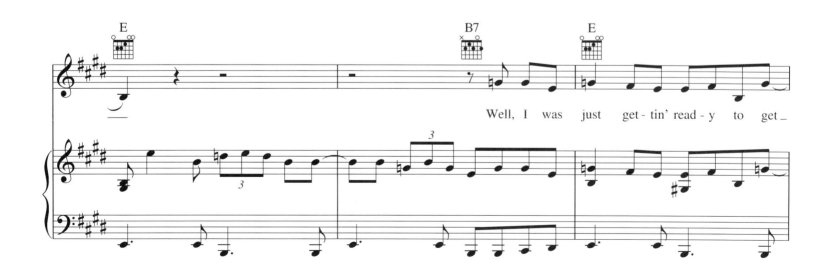

© 1972 (Renewed 2000) TIME IN A BOTTLE PUBLISHING and CROCE PUBLISHING
All Rights Controlled and Administered by EMI APRIL MUSIC INC.
All Rights Reserved   International Copyright Secured   Used by Permission

Additional Lyrics

2. She's a-five foot six and two fifteen,
   A bleached blonde mama with a streak of mean;
   She knew how to knuckle
   And she knew how to scuffle and fight.
   And the roller derby program said
   That she were built like a 'frigerator with a head,
   The fans called her "Tuffy,"
   But all her buddies called her "Spike."
   Chorus

3. Well, I could not help but fall in love
   With this heavy duty woman I been speakin' of;
   Things looked kind of bad
   Until the day she skated into my life.
   Well, she might be nasty, she might be fat,
   But I never met a person who would tell her that;
   She's my big blonde bomber,
   My heavy-handed Hackensack Mama.
   Chorus

SPEEDBALL TUCKER

Words and Music by
JIM CROCE

Additional Lyrics

3. One day I looked into my rearview mirror
   And a-comin' up from behind
   There was a Georgia State policeman
   And a hundred dollar fine.
   Well, he looked me in the eye as he was writin' me up
   And said, "Driver, you been flyin'
   And ninety-five was the route you were on.
   It was not the speed limit sign."
   Chorus

THESE DREAMS

Words and Music by
JIM CROCE

VESPERS

Words and Music by JIM CROCE and INGRID CROCE

TOP HAT BAR AND GRILLE

Words and Music by
JIM CROCE

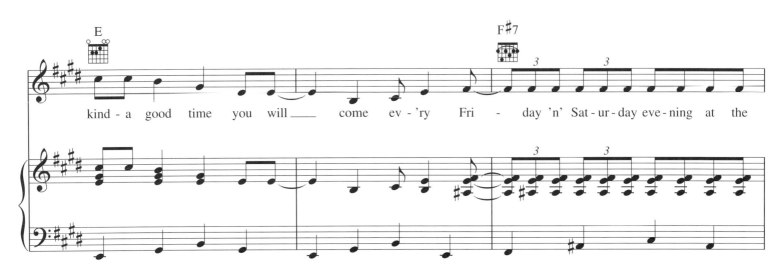

© 1973 (Renewed 2001) TIME IN A BOTTLE PUBLISHING and CROCE PUBLISHING
All Rights Controlled and Administered by EMI APRIL MUSIC INC.
All Rights Reserved International Copyright Secured Used by Permission

WALKIN' BACK TO GEORGIA

Words and Music by
JIM CROCE

© 1971 (Renewed 1999) TIME IN A BOTTLE PUBLISHING and CROCE PUBLISHING
All Rights Controlled and Administered by EMI APRIL MUSIC INC.
All Rights Reserved   International Copyright Secured   Used by Permission

WHICH WAY ARE YOU GOIN'

Words and Music by JIM CROCE
and INGRID CROCE

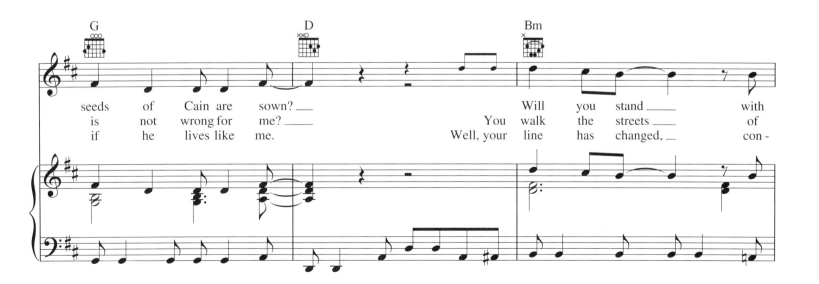

© 1975 (Renewed 2003) TIME IN A BOTTLE PUBLISHING and CROCE PUBLISHING
All Rights Controlled and Administered by EMI APRIL MUSIC INC.
All Rights Reserved   International Copyright Secured   Used by Permission

WORKIN' AT THE CAR WASH BLUES

Words and Music by
JIM CROCE

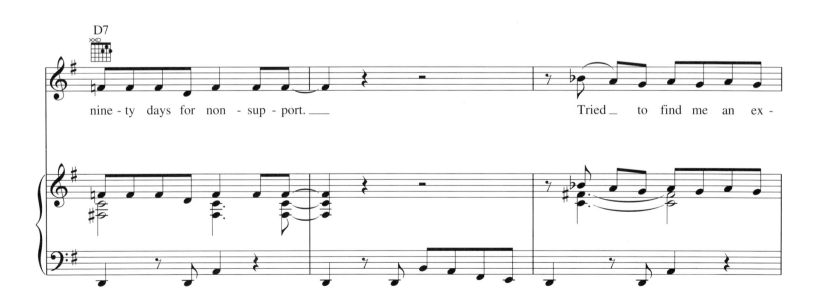

Well, I had just got out from the county pris-on, doin' nine-ty days for non-sup-port. Tried to find me an ex-

© 1973 (Renewed 2001) TIME IN A BOTTLE PUBLISHING and CROCE PUBLISHING
All Rights Controlled and Administered by EMI APRIL MUSIC INC.
All Rights Reserved International Copyright Secured Used by Permission

YOU DON'T MESS AROUND WITH JIM

Words and Music by
JIM CROCE

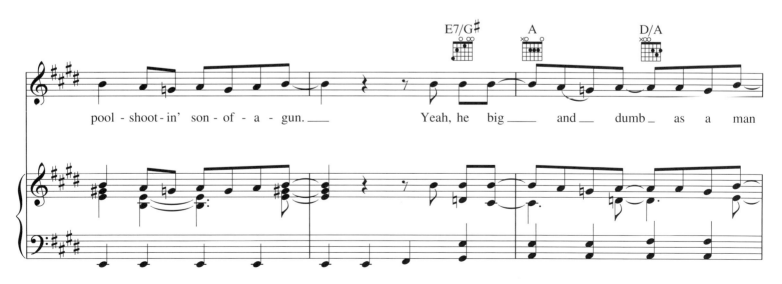

© 1971 (Renewed 1999) TIME IN A BOTTLE PUBLISHING and CROCE PUBLISHING
All Rights Controlled and Administered by EMI APRIL MUSIC INC.
All Rights Reserved International Copyright Secured Used by Permission

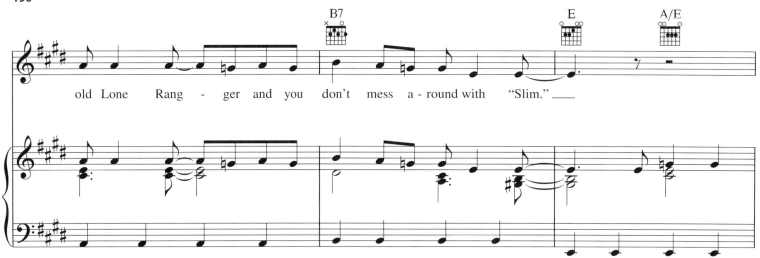

old Lone Rang - ger and you don't mess a - round with "Slim." ___

(Spoken:) Yeah, big Jim got his hat, find out
Even if you do got a two - piece custom - made pool cue.

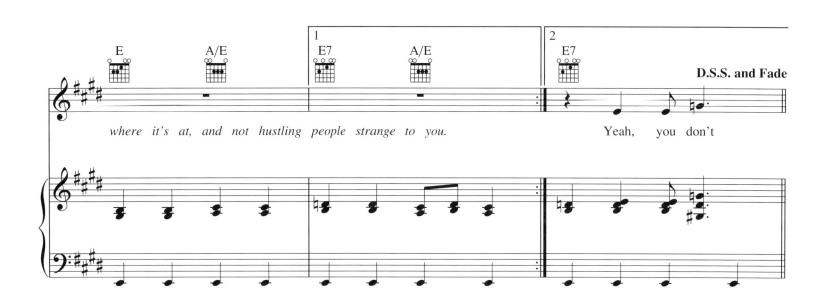

where it's at, and not hustling people strange to you. Yeah, you don't

D.S.S. and Fade

Dear Jay —

Thanks for letting me sit in your car. If you ever get to Phila. I'll let you sit in my truck

thanks

Jim Croce

Jim's handwritten note to Jay Morgenstern, Vice-President of ABC Records, 1973